Overcoming Homelessness

instagram! @ homelessliues matter book

Venmo: @ Leo-Gnaua

Hi neighbor!

My friend Leo is an incredible human with an inspiring story. I hope you enjoy his book!

Overcoming Homelessness

My Personal Story

Leo Gnawa

Self-Published -By-Leo Gnawa

Copyright ©2023 Leo Gnawa

All rights reserved

No part of this book may be reproduced, stored in a retrieval system, or transmitted in any form, of by any means, electronic, mechanical, photocopying, recording or otherwise. Without prior permission of the publisher.

First Edition

ISBN: 9798390315002

I dedicate this book to Jasmine Flowers, a young lady that I met while selling my books on the streets and who I adopted as my daughter. She's Been there for me since.

TABLE OF CONTENTS:

Chapter 1: Having Same Dreams And Nightmares ---Page 1

Chapter 2: Turning My Nightmares Into A Better Dream---Page 13

Chapter 3: Surviving Through Calamities---Page 33

Chapter 4: I turned Bad Luck Into Good Luck---Page 55

Chapter 5: I Got Out Of Homelessness By Working For Myself --Page 73

Chapter 6: Selling My Books To Keep A Roof Over My Head----Page 85

Chapter 7: Being Tolerant Because of Bad Experiences---103

Chapter 8: Getting Put Out And Don't Know What To Do---135

INTRODUCTION:

I wrote this book to share my story about how I got myself out of homelessness. As a self-published anti-homelessness activist-author, my mission is to create awareness about homelessness so that we can end homelessness.

I personally have experienced chronic homelessness off and on for twenty and plus years in the Washington DC area. I shared my experience with homelessness while trying to create awareness about homelessness, in my first book titled Homeless Lives Matter, Homeless My story.

Yes, I know, being homeless for twenty and plus years is a long time, although actually I was able to find a room for rent or stay with friends, many times during those years. So, I was not homeless living outside or in shelters, for twenty straight years although I did for most of those years. But I still considered myself a chronic homeless person.

About two years ago, precisely in February 2021, I successfully got myself out of homelessness on my own and have been able to keep renting a place and pay rent from my own pocket. It has not been easy but am still trying hard to keep a roof over my head and not be homeless again.

I even wrote a second book titled Survival And Life, The Lessons I learned. I wanted to inspire and motivate others to try their best to deal with and overcome adversities by sharing some of the lessons I learned through my experience with homelessness. This book, Overcoming Homelessness, My Personal Story is more about how I got myself out of homelessness. So, it is purposed to accomplish both goals of my two previous books. I believe that we can end homelessness and we should. I know how traumatic homelessness is and has been in my case and how it feels to no longer be homeless. I don't know how as a society, we can and will end homelessness. But I can at least share with you how I personally did it for myself. I sincerely hope that this book will inspire you to commit to the cause of ending homelessness or at least motivate you to help somebody get out of homelessness. Let's end homeless. Leo

CHAPTER I

HAVING SAME WEIRD DREAMS AND NIGHTMARES

When I was still living in a tent in the bushes, I used to go to a friend's house and sleep on his couch or floor when it was too cold to sleep in my tent during the winter. That was during the pandemic, but towards the end of it. From the start of the pandemic up to 4 months into it, I stayed in my tent and never went inside anybody's house.

I met him on the streets when he was homeless also. I have known him for decades. I think he was homeless for at least twenty years if I am not mistaken. He used to sleep in a doorway of a building on Pennsylvania Avenue, not far from the US capitol. He received his apartment through a Washington DC program to house the homeless who met the requirements for free housing. He told me that I could come and spend a night at his place, anytime I felt the need to be inside when the weather was inclement. I first started going there to take a shower, whenever I could not make it to the regular places offering free showers to the homeless. But whenever I got very cold in my tent in the winter, I called him and asked if I could come there for a night or two. He never said no. I rode my bike from my tent on North Capitol Street to his place near the Trinidad neighborhood of Northeast Washington DC. I made it a habit to offer him $20 for the night that I spent there, although he never asked me for anything. I did that because I wanted him to know that I appreciated that he let me come and sleep in his living room and turn it into my living space for a night or couples of nights that I used to spend there. I felt very comfortable going there because he let me have my space his living room), and some quietness and peace of mind. He even allowed me to order my books to his address. I even paid him a few times to go ship my books for me when I had a lot of orders to ship at one time.

One thing I noticed about him that kind of disturbed me at first, was that he spent his entire day in his bedroom, either sleeping, or watching old western movies when he was awakened. He would get up, fix something to eat, go back to his bedroom, watch television, and go back to sleep. I noticed him doing it for months and months for the four to five years that he got housed. I could never understand why anyone wanted to just sleep day and night and night and day every day. But I will be honest, I found myself doing the same thing when I got my own place. I was fortunate enough to be able to sell enough books online to cover my rent every month for the two years that I was in my first place, after being homeless for twenty and some years off and on, off course. I cannot describe the great sense of relief that I felt when just lying in my own bed and being in my own space for the first time, in such a long time. It seems like my body was just healing from decades of sleeping on benches on the streets, on bunk beds at shelters, or on the floor in somebody's home. It was then easier for me to understand my friend. He had been sleeping outside on the concrete ground in a doorway for years and years.

I am still having nightmares in my sleep up to today, two years after I got out of homelessness.

That speaks volume of the trauma that homelessness has been for me and how is still affecting me, two years after although I have a roof over my head now.

What are These Strange dreams About?

I was on a bus, heading to an unknown destination and coming from a place that I could not remember. I got out of the bus by a mall, when it reached its final destination. I stood at a phone booth. I have no idea which city I was in, why I was there and where to go there and from there. I looked back at the bus and thought about getting back on it, but I had no idea where I was trying to go back to. I was in a state of confusion. I closed my eyes and try to wake myself up. I woke up in my tent on my bed very confused but relieved that it was just a dream.

I had several same dreams. In most of them, I was finding myself in a city and feeling lost with no money and not knowing what to do and where to go. In many of the dreams, I walked around and realized that I had no shoes on. I felt very embarrassed and worried. But what I found very strange is that, within the dream, when my anxiety and stress was becoming unbearable, I started wondering in the dream whether this was a dream of real? I always was able to become conscious in my dream and close my eyes in the dream and force myself to wake up. And I woke up on my bed in the tent and sat on it and tried to process what the dream was all about.

I had a bed in my tent. My tent was located in the bushes off North Capitol Street by the little bridge going over Irving Street, and surrounded by some exits to and from North Capitol street. One night, about 2 or 3 am, I heard a loud noise while I was inside the tent. I waited till a bit before sunrise to step out and check what it was that was thrown out there, most likely from a vehicle. I saw a large mattress and a spring box. I dragged them into my tent. That is how I ended up having a bed inside. The bed was very comfortable, but I was still having nightmares back-to-back to the point that I was anxious to go back to sleep after waking up from a nightmare.

In another similar dream that I had multiple times also, I got to a town, checked in a hotel and stepped out of the room to go to a place that I did not know. When I came back to the hotel, I walked by the main office but could not remember which room I was in. After walking around, I tried to get back to the hotel lobby, but kept walking by several buildings and could never get to the lobby. In another version of the same dream, it seemed like the more I walked around, the more rooms appeared. I found myself like in a labyrinth. I was just walking in circle and unable to recognize which one of the rooms was mine. The more I walked around, the more rooms popped up. I got so confused and woke myself up. I had the same dream countless times. The hotels were different, and the environment was not the same, but it was the same story.

I had gotten me a nice apartment and was very happy. One day I tried to go home but got into the building and could not remember which of the apartments in there was mine. I became very sad and kept walking around. I woke up in my tent and faced the reality of me being a homeless living in a tent, in the bushes.

I was in an elevator trying to get to a floor up, but the elevator kept going very fast up and speeding up without stopping, until I started worrying. The elevator kept speeding up like a rocket. I did not know whether it was going to stop or burst out into the sky. I suddenly woke up and sat on my bed in the tent as usual, trying to understand that dream also. I had the same dream many times also.

I was walking down the street and found myself in an emergency situation. I or somebody else felt threatened by someone or a group of individuals. I needed to call the police urgently. I walked around trying to find a payphone to call for emergency but to no avail. or I had a phone but tried to make the call but it has not going through. I was getting impatient. I kept walking around but still could not find someone with a phone to call emergency for me, until I woke myself up before I got hurt. I had the same dream many times.

I went to the Safeway on New York Avenue to get some food to eat before heading to the corner on the street where I sell my books. I got some fruits mostly. I rode my bike to the Church on the corner of Massachusetts Avenue and 9th street or 9th and

HAVING SAME WEIRD DREAMS AND HIGHTMARES

K. I rode inside the park. It is separated from the church by a fence lined up with bushes on both sides. The park was turned into a homeless camp. There were about 20 tents inside. I had a cart tied to the back of my bike. I had my books in the cart. I sat on the steps on the south side of the church, on the side of K street. As a matter of fact, my true intention was to take some of my books that I had stashed in the bushes. But I did not want any of the homeless and folks in the park to see me getting the books out the bushes. I did not want anyone to know that I had stashed some of my books there. I wanted to retrieve them when I was sure that nobody watched me doing so. So, I got my food out of my backpack after laying my bike on the sidewalk. Before I had a chance to eat my food, a stocky guy with another one who was slim and taller, walked from the park towards me. "Hey, get your bike off the sidewalk" he yelled. I thought it was kind of rude for him to address me like that. But I thought he was a homeless guy that I knew, and who had the tendency to joke with me by being rude and condescending. So, I responded to him by telling him to fly over the bike. I realized that he wasn't the person I thought he was, when he and his friend walked towards me.

He was very infuriated. Both of them stood on the steps in front of me while I was in a sitting position on the lower steps. The shorter guy acted like he was about to attack me. He actually told his friend" Let's get this work". I took it to mean, let's attack him. This was not a dream. It was real. But the first thing I thought about was the dream that I had many times, in which I was caught off guard by attackers but woke myself up before they attacked me. Many a time, when I was having those dreams, I sat on my bed and wondered how I would have handled such a situation in real life. Now this was happening to me, and I was totally unprepared. I normally would always get myself in a defensive position whenever I sensed danger, and I would not let anybody get that close to me. I normally would stand up and make sure that there is a distance between me and anybody who I perceive as a threat or potential threat. But, this time, I sat there and let those two guys get too close to me. I was sitting down, and they were standing. The first thing I thought about was grabbing a knife that I kept in my backpack sometimes. When I put my hand in my backpack, the two guys moved back. But I was out of luck. I could not feel the knife in my backpack. One of the guys reached out to something under around his belt and never pulled it out. I don't think it was a gun, but I have no clue what it was whatever it was. The next thing I thought about was my phone. But I rose up so to not allow them to hit me since they wanted to attack me. I stood up, they backed off but were still in close distance. I got my phone out of my pocket. The shorter guy tried to slap it off my hand because he knew that I wanted to call the police. But my phone was still in my hand. He then called out few names of some guys in the camp in the park. Four to five of them ran out of the park towards us. Some of them grabbed some sticks and poles. I got a bit worried because I was outnumbered. I tried to defuse the situation by telling the guy that I thought he was someone I knew. But he kept ordering me to get my bike and leave. Although I was surrounded by him and his crew, I still did not show any fear. I kept asking him why was he acting like that? The reality of it is that I did not want to be punked. So, I stood there not sure what to do. But I thought bending down and grabbing my bike was a bad idea. I could be jumped when leaning down. One of the guys, who came with the group from the park, grabbed my back and set it against an electric pole. I reached into my pocket again and got my phone out. I wanted to call the police. The short guy slapped my hand. My phone fell. I rushed down to pick it. I was surrounded by four or five guys and did not want any of them to pick up my phone from the ground and run with it. But as soon as I bent down, the stocky guy ordered his guys to attack me. I felt a lot of punches in my face coming from all directions in a few seconds. I stood right up. They stopped jumping me and backed off. I reached inside my mouth and pulled a broken tooth and showed it to them. "You broke my tooth," I said. My mouth was bloodied. My lips were swollen and busted. I had blood all over my shirt. I dialed 911. The attackers dispersed while I was making the call. I stood there until three police cars pulled up within five minutes. When the officers asked me to identify them, I could only describe the two who started the whole situation. But, honest truth, I could not remember what the other four who joined looked like. I did not even know who exactly hit me. The punches were coming from my side and from behind me. My face was facing the ground because I still bent from picking up my phone. The police officers were not being friendly to me. I was irritated and could not tell them who exact hit me. But I assumed that the two guys who started it did hit me. An ambulance showed up, but I refused to go to the hospital. I had a broker tooth, some cuts on my lips and some wounds inside my mouth. I also had two teeth that was shaken. I ended up going to the dentist the next morning and got four teeth pulled out of my mouth, including the piece that remained from the broken tooth. A couple of days after the attack, I was told by some homeless acquaintances that the main culprit of the attack was a drug dealer who had set up shop in the homeless camp in that park. He was from a neighborhood, few blocks from the downtown area of Washington DC in the northwest part of town. Obviously, he was monitoring everything that was moving around the park because he was conducting his business there in broad daylight. He probably noticed me sitting on the steps near the park while he was monitoring every movement in and around the park. He though my bike on the sidewalk was drawing attention, I guess. Or he was just in the illusion that he was the lord of the area and had the right to decide who sits or hangs around there. Obviously, he had people coming in and out of the park to buy drugs, but nobody could notice, unless they were hanging around and watching what was happening in the park. I knew that some young folks from nearby neighborhoods were coming to hustle in some of the homeless guys' tents and using some of the homeless in the camp, to sell their stuff in their tent. But I had no idea who this guy was and what he was doing there. I was only around to get my books that I had stashed in the bushes nearby, and also eat my food before heading to my spot, where I sell my books. I heard that a park police officer arrested him few days after the incident. The arrest was unrelated to the attack on me. The park police officers arrested him on suspicion of drug dealing in the park. I heard that he got released but rearrested few days later by that same officer. But he got out again and stopped hustling in and around that park. They probably did not find any drug on him although they probably have been watching him and knew what he was coming to that park for. Few weeks later, that park was shut down. All the tents were removed, and the camp is still shut down up to today. I wrote about this incident to make a point. I had several nightmares in my tent about being attacked by surprise and not knowing what to do. I woke up from the dreams and wondered what I would have done in real life situations like that. I always told myself that I will always be prepared to deal with surprise attacks. But I got caught off guard that time.

I ordered a hunter knife and pepper gel spray online after that incident. But honest truth, I rarely carry them with me when I go out. I used to when I first got them. But now, I don't any more. I just try to avoid putting myself into a vulnerable position and getting caught off guard.

I had been homeless for a long time but never been jumped or violently attacked by surprise. I stayed in a tent in the woods by myself but never felt afraid or in harm's way. At night, the area where my tent was located was pitch dark. I never had any light in my tent. I was just staying in the dark in my tent under a tree surrounded by trees and tall grass and bushes. There were street lights around and a road nearby. But there was nobody walking around there, except few rare occasions. I had a long metal bar that was heavy enough to inflict lethal damage to any human or animal trying to attack me. That was the only weapon I had. The only time I held it ready to use it to defend my self is when I spotted a wild dog, a coyote most likely, coming out of the woods nearby towards my tent, but not sure whether to come closer. I had got some fried fish on my way to my tent. I sat on a chair outside the tent and got the fish out of the box in the dark. The coyote probably smelled the fish from its position in the woods. I grabbed the metal pole and stood up. The coyote kept moving back and forth from the wood half way to my tent, then just run back down the exit road towards the east of me, along the bushes by the fence of the Old Soldiers Home golf course. When I was assured that the animal had gone far enough, I sat down on the chair and ate my fish. I entered my tent and got me a good sleep after I finished eating. A few other times, I grabbed my metal pole and looked outside my tent in the dark, when I was awakened by some approaching noise. When I opened the tent and looked outside, I saw some glittering eyes in the dark. I used my phone flashlight to see what it was. It was a raccoon. I made some noise to chase it away. It ran away. I went back to sleep undisturbed.

Now let's get back to more of my dreams or nightmares shall I say.

I was walking in woods or residential areas sometimes, and whenever I sensed danger, I jumped in the air and started flying like a bird and could not control my flight and stop whenever I wanted to. I told myself during the dream that I must be dreaming and forced myself to wake up. I sat on my bed and was confused as usual whenever I keep having those weird dreams. I coincidentally felt like my luck was bad at the time when those dreams were recurrent.

I was walking in woods and residential areas sometimes, and whenever I sensed danger or wanted to show that I could escape anytime, I jumped up in the sky above trees and flew away from the danger and could stop my flight anytime I desired to. When I started having those dreams regularly instead of the other ones, I felt like my luck was going to be good from that time on.

I was in a jail cell. The door was unlocked. I was alone. There was a lobby behind an open door near the cell. Someone came to the front desk in the lobby. I was called up there. I walked out of the cell. A lady was at the desk and a prison guard was sitting at the desk. I picked up some boxes to help the lady at the desk carry them to her car that was parked in a yard outside of the jail. After I put the box in her car trunk, and was about to walk back to my cell, she asked me what I wanted to do. Either go with her or return to the cell? I was confused because it seemed like I could, on my free will, either go with her, or return to my cell. Nobody was there to prevent me from leaving with her or force me back into the cell. But I was ambivalent between the desire to go free and the fear of getting in trouble if I leave the jail. Before I decided what to do, I woke up on my bed totally confused and trying to understand the dream. I only add that dream one time, but I am still puzzled by it even today.

One day, while we were into a group conversation at Father Mc Kenna center where I went to take a shower, I shared the dream with the 5 or 6 homeless guys in the group, and the moderator who was a former catholic priest and a volunteer at the center. According to him, the dream meant that I was keeping myself homeless and could get myself out of it if I chose to.

His interpretation of my dream got me cogitating seriously on the point he made although I was not really in agreement with him.

CHAPTER 2

TURNING MY NIGHTMARES INTO A BETTER DREAM

(I learned from nightmares instead of being stressed by them)

I woke up from another of my weird dreams and nightmares and sat on my bed in my tent and felt depressed about being homeless for so long and not seeing any end to it. Sometimes, I had good dreams. In some of them, I was living in an ideal multilevel house that was mine but had to wake up to reality as a homeless man in a tent in the bushes.

I can say that stress and depression contributed to me staying homeless for so long. I was allowing the problems that I had to overwhelm me. My thinking was clouded by anxiety and depression and hopelessness because I was constantly worried and stressed out.

When your mind is constantly worrying, you are not able to focus on solving problems. That was my reality for so long.

I realized that spending too much time worrying myself too much instead of focusing on finding a solution to whatever problem I was facing, was causing me to be stressed out and depressed and not helping me at all.

While laying on that mattress and feeling stressed out, I told myself," Leo, you are a very intelligent man, why aren't you using your intelligence to figure a way out of this situation you are in?"

I decided to stop spending too much time worrying and started focusing on a way out. That was to me the start of the process of figuring out a way of getting out of homelessness. I decided to write books and sell them to make enough money to afford a roof over my head. I figured out a way to get enough money to afford a laptop and use it to write my first book. I went on the street and panhandled around the holiday season. I knew from other homeless folks who panhandled that people were very generous during the holiday season. I knew it was a degrading thing to do, but I swallowed my pride and went out there and begged for money and saved most of it. A month later, precisely a day or two after New Year's day of January 2015, I went to a computer store in Virginia and got me a laptop. I spent the whole year writing while staying in a tent. Sometimes it was freezing cold in the tent. The temperature was below freezing. But whenever I felt inspired in the middle of the night, I came out from under my pile of blankets and covers, totally ignored how cold my fingers were and pulled my laptop and typed to write my book. When I could barely feel and move my frozen fingers, I tucked both hands between my thighs under the covers and rubbed them against each other to warm them up and resumed writing when I could feel them.

OVERCOMING HOMELESSNESS

I wrote my first book, Homeless Lives Matter, Homeless My story under rough conditions. I finished and self-published it in 2016. But it took me another year to really start selling it on the street in front of Old Ebbits Grill. It is known as the oldest restaurant in Washington DC. It is located on 15th Street, between F and G streets, right across the Treasury Department which is on the left hand of the White House. It also has bars in it that are open until 2 pm every night.

I started selling them in the afternoon until late at night, sometime until 2 am. I sold them for $10 a copy on the street although the price on amazon was $15. I averaged two sales per hour daily. I used a carboard box to sit my books on and made some signs with foam boards and markers that I purchased at CVS.

Later on, I started using professionally made posters at a Staple Store that was located on the corner of H and 13th street, in North West Washington DC. The location is now a 24-hour Wawa convenient store. A lady who purchased my book one day, when she walked by me to her office nearby, had my first signs made and brought them to me. I stashed the signs in a back alley whenever I finished selling my books. I could not take my signs with me to my tent. I had too much to carry with me and my tent was a bit far away. I had to ride my bike for 30 minutes before getting to my tent. I carried my books on my back in an army duffel bag every day, from my tent to downtown back and forth. I ended up injuring my shoulder. I never knew that shoulder pain was so excruciating. The pain lasted for a couple of weeks. Because of the shoulder pain, I started stashing my books in bushes downtown, by the church on the corner of K and 9th Street, in North West Washington DC. I knew a couple of homeless guys who were sleeping on top of the steps in front of the Church entrance doors. One of them called me one afternoon and told me that a crew of the Downtown Service cleaned the bushes and removed my books from there. I had a box containing about 100 books in it. I did not come out to sell books the day before that day. The homeless folks who were sleeping around the church, used to stash their belongings in the bushes. I was in my tent. I got on my bike and rushed downtown. My books were gone when I searched the bushes where they were hidden. I panicked and rode my bike to the office of the Downtown DC cleaning crew by the Mc Donald on 13th and New York Avenue. I noticed a few copies of my book on some of the tables in the main office. I found out that my books were found by the folks who cleaned the park. But I was told that they threw the entire box away because the books were wet. I thought that was some lie. I had put the box in a plastic trash bag and tied it up before hiding it in the bushes. I had just received the box which was delivered to the nearby office of a person who looked out for me. I think the guys who found the book took the box home with them after sharing few copies with folks who were in the office. I was given all the copies that were found in the office. They were less than twenty. It was a big loss for a homeless man who is selling his book to take care of himself out there. That was about $1000 that I could have made from the books that I lost.

But I did not let that incident discourage me. I kept ordering more books with the little money that I had and selling them on the street. My goal was to save enough money to get a place one day, but after two years of selling my books on the streets, I had not saved enough money to secure a roof over my head.

OVERCOMING HOMELESSNESS

Being A Good Samaritan While Homeless Myself

While I was homeless myself, I didn't mind using a lot of the money I made selling my books, to help many street acquaintances who were single mothers and had problems paying their phone their rent, phone bills, or put food in their fridge.

I was standing by the steps of the church while talking to a homeless lady that I was acquainted with. It was a Sunday around 8 am. The church was doing showers for the homeless and also offering breakfast in the basement of the church. I was about to enter the room and ask who the last person was who was waiting to get in the next available showers. There were two separate bathrooms for male and female. Each had three showers. There was no list to sign. The showers were open to the next person who was waiting. So, whoever wanted to take a shower had to ask for who was waiting next and then go after him when the next shower open. Some of the guys were staying in the shower as long as they wanted without any consideration for those waiting. But everybody waiting was able to get in within the two hours that the place was open for showers. I think it was from 8;00am to 10:00am.

A lady was standing next to the one I was talking to. I knew she was not homeless, and she was not there for shower either. She was coming there for coffee. They did not serve a full breakfast, but they had some coffee, tea and bagels and also were giving out toiletries and undergarments for men and women. It was obvious to me that she was that wherever she was staying was not her own place.

I told the lady I was talking to, that I had terrible shoulder pain. The lady next to her jumped into the conversation and said that she had some pain killer on her dresser and would have brought them if she had known. I was touched by her concern although I never interacted with her before. A week later, on a Sunday also, she was at the door of the side of the church basement, when I came there to take a shower. I had ridden my bicycle from my tent to the church in order to shower. I did not care much about the pastries and coffee that they were offering. She looked so disturbed. I asked her if she was ok. She nodded and started shedding tears. I asked her what was wrong. She told me that she was tired of not having her own and not being able to provide for her son. She said that she was staying with her grandmother in a subsidized apartment few blocks from where we were. Another male cousin of her was also staying there. No one else was supposed to live in the apartment except her grandmother. She said that the male cousin was giving her a hard time and trying to cause her to get put out of there. She also said that her son was staying with her uncle, but the uncle had a wife who did not allow her to go to their apartment to see her son. She felt that the uncle's wife had more control over her son than she, the mother. She could only see her son when she sees him outside. The uncle did not have legal custody of the son. So, the son was just staying there because the mother had no place of her own to take him in. She kept crying the more she explained the situation to me. I know she had a drug addiction issue because I have seen her with her boyfriend getting high on in the park many times. I found out later that she was getting high on PCP and also on K2 spice. But I did not know if her problem was due to her drug problems are not. I asked her why she did not apply for free housing, since she was a single mother of a boy who was about ten-year-old. She told me that she did not have a phone to keep in touch with social workers and the proper agencies that could help her go through the process of getting a place. I remembered the morning that she showed some concern about my shoulder pain and thought about sharing her painkillers with me. I wanted to help to because of that to show my gratitude for her empathy.

I told her that if she promised me that she would go to an agency which helps single homeless mothers like her get into free housing, I would buy her a phone and pay the phone bill for the following three months. She was surprised but accepted. I told her to meet me at the metro PCS store on North Capitol Street the next day. I had a Metro PCS phone service (now Metro By Two Mobile). She showed up and I got her a phone and put her added a second line to my service for her. I got disappointed at her because a couple of months has passed, and she still made no real effort to get into housing. I threatened to stop paying her bill and I did.

She reached back to me and asked me to give her a second chance. She claimed that she had enrolled into a drug program treatment and wanted me to keep her phone on until she gets out the program, follows up with her case manager at the agency and gets into housing. I got her back on my phone bill plan so that she could keep her number. She went into the program for few months and came back and got temporarily housed into a hotel, while waiting for permanent housing. She took her son with her, and they stayed together in the hotel room paid by the agency until they got them an apartment. I was still homeless and living in my tent in the woods. She never called me to tell me that I could come and take a shower at her hotel room when her son was in school. But I did not care about that. I was happy I helped get in the process of having free housing for her and her son.

I am not expecting any reciprocation from anybody that I help even if they end up doing better than I. I am just happy for them and grateful for the opportunity I had to help somebody. The good you put out there always come back as good luck. So, I believe.

She ended up losing the phone I got her and got herself another phone and found a way to get her phone bill paid. She did not keep in touch or call me to say thank you, Leo, for everything you did for me, or let me know that she finally got into permanent housing for her and her son.

I had gone to Walmart on H Street about a year later and run through her. I was a bit upset. She gave me some bogus reasons why she did not get in touch or at least call me to let me know that she had finally got housed. She asked me for some money, I told her that she had been ungrateful and didn't appreciate what I did for her. She got upset and called me "a homeless bum". That really hurts my feelings. I helped that lady a whole lot when she was homeless herself.

One time, I was staying at a friend's girlfriend apartment temporarily when she was in the process of moving to another apartment. In the meantime, she was staying at her boyfriend's, my friend's place and was rarely going to her apartment. The apartment was on Hawaii Avenue, North East, right off North Capitol Street, about ten minutes' walk from my tent which was also few blocks south off North Capitol. I stayed there for about a month, but I still kept all my belongings in my tent. The lady I was talking about called me one day in tears. I asked her what was wrong. She told me that she had got put out of her grandmother's place because a person in the property rental management had put her out her grandmother apartment when they saw her there. She was barred from the premises and was not supposed to be there. Her grandmother could no longer let her sneak in there anymore. She herself could be evicted from there if she kept allowing her niece in her apartment.

She had nowhere to go. I felt sorry for her when hearing her crying hysterically on the phone. I told her that I was staying at a friend's place, and she could come stay with me there at night when I finish selling my books, but she had to leave in the morning before the rental office opened. I wasn't supposed to stay there, and I didn't want my friend's girlfriend, who let me stay there, find out that I was taking someone there. You can imagine how shocked and hurt I was, when a person calls me a homeless bum after she got a place and forgot all I did to help her when she was homeless herself.

But this did not deter me from helping others. I am not trying to brag about what I do for others. I am only making the point that no matter what hardship I am in, I still have empathy and show compassion for others who are going through similar or even worse situations than what I am going through.

I will give another example. I was helping this lady that I used to see all the time around SOME area. She was not homeless, but she was a poor person who was living in a subsidized building around the corner on North Capitol. That means that her rent, like anybody else in the building, was paid by the government. She was walking with her friend and stopped by me to ask me if I could spare a cigarette. That was a slang expression meaning, do you have an extra cigarette that you can give me?

I told her that I didn't smoke cigarettes, but I gave her a couple of dollars instead. She thanked me and left with her friend. A couple of days later, I was standing outside of SOME and about to lock my bike to the rail, by the door at the entrance of the dining room and go sign the shower list. She was there to get some coffee. She was coming from time to time get some coffee at SOME during breakfast time. She walked up to me with her abnormal walking. Later on, she told me that she walked like that because she got shot in the leg few years ago. Anyway, she asked me for my number because she wanted to stay in touch. I told her to hold on while I leaned to lock my bike. I gave her my number. She asked me to buy her breakfast at Mc Donald, few blocks from there. I gave her $10 to get herself some breakfast, although she could have got free breakfast right there where we were at SOME. But she said that she only came for coffee and wanted me to get some breakfast at Mc Donald for her and her daughter. When she mentioned her daughter, I did not hesitate to give her some money so she could get some to eat at Mc Donald for her and her daughter. Since then, she had been calling me a lot to ask me to buy her and her daughter some breakfast or some groceries when they did not have enough food at home. Sometimes I was in my tent, but most the time, I was at my friend's place in the Trinidad neighborhood. It was going to his place when it was too cold in my tent. That was in the winter of 2020. I used to ride my bike from his place to my spot downtown to sell my books. I would tell her to meet me at the Mc Donald on New York Avenue not far from her building on North Capitol, or at the Denny's that was on the corner of Florida Avenue and North Capitol. I used to ride my bike through the area on my way to sell my books. I asked her to meet me at the Safeway on 5th and K street NW, or the Walmart on H street, NW, when I could help her with groceries. Although I liked her and she pretended to like me, we never had any intimate physical contact. I was just helping her out of kindness of heart for the most part. But one time, I saw her walking with a guy towards her building, and she stopped talking to me. She asked me for some money. I joked with her "how can you be with a man and ask me for some money? Your man supposed to take care of you, not me". She answered that he was the best friend of her deceased brother and that he was just a friend. He stepped away from us while waiting for her ahead of us. I suspected that she was lying and that the guy was her boyfriend. I felt like, if she has a man who stays with her, that is his responsibility to take care of her, not mine. I don't mind helping a lady who is a single mother and is poor and in need of help. But I don't think it is fair for me to take care of somebody else's girlfriend unless she is in an abusive situation and needs some help get out of the toxic relationship. Some people take other people kindness for stupidity, and I don't want to be the victim of such people who only see a kind person as someone to be taken advantage of.

One evening, I saw her with the same guy getting off their bicycles to get inside the Walmart on H Street, North West. I was about to enter the store, after I locked my bike where they were about to lock theirs. It was now obvious to me that the guy was her boyfriend and that most likely he lived with her in her apartment. She said Hi to me, I responded and went into the store. She had not been calling me for months after I last saw her. One day, I got on the 92 bus on Florida Avenue. She was on the bus. She got off her seat and came to sit next to me. Leo, "I need some help. I don't have any food in my house". Can I get some money?" I looked at her and told her, "You want to be with a man who can't do nothing for you, but you have him stay in your house, and you come and ask me to take care of you. Do I look like I am stupid? I am not your man. Go ask the man who is staying with you, and who you sleep with to feed you. I am not your man" She burst out laughing". Her stop was next, she kept saying, "come on Leo please, I need some money. I need to get some food." I pulled five dollars' out of my pocket and gave it to her and told her sarcastically "that is all I can do for you".

I met her another time on North Capitol Street. She asked me for money to get a sandwich at the Chinese Food Carry out across the street. She also told me that she needed a phone, because her daughter had left the apartment with her phone, since they were sharing the phone together. I told her that I am not taking care of anybody's girlfriend. "I'm by myself, Ain't got no man" she responded. "Stop lying. You think I am stupid? I know the guy I saw you with a few times, and the last time at Walmart while you guys were on the bike, is your man and staying with you", I said back to her.

She told me that she had enough of him and put him out because he was no help to her. All he was doing was having too much sex with her as if he was trying to get her pregnant according to what she told me. Honest truth, my pride as a man was kind of hurt. I told myself, "she knows I like her, and she pretends to like me, but she never really showed any serious desire to be with me". Yet, she acted like I was her man, only when she wanted some money or help from me. Yet, she was involved in a relationship with somebody who was staying with her and not doing much for her. I felt like I was being used and taken advantage of like a sugar daddy who never got the booty and whose kindness was being taken for stupidity.

I have been there for her for the couple of years I have known her, but she never really acted like she wanted to be in a relationship with me. The feeling of rejection that I was getting made me feel like she only wanted to use me because she knew I liked her, and she only saw me as someone she could get whatever she wanted out of, by pretending that she liked me and wanted to be with me. I told her that I had no problem helping her from time to time when I could, but I could not take care of her as if she was my woman. "You don't want me," she said. I laughed. "Well, you ain't ready for me. I said in a joking manner." I am! I am serious!" she responded.

I felt flattered but was not interested in being into a relationship with her, to be honest. I found her attractive physically, but I was looking for more than physical attractiveness in a mate.

She came and visited me a couple of times at my friend's place in 2020, and also later, in my first apartment in 2021 and 2022, and spent the night there. She woke up in my bed in the morning in her underwear. She was happy and relaxed. "I needed to get away from over there for a minute", she said. It has always been too much going on in the housing project building on the corner of North Capital and New York Avenue and the whole neighborhood where she lives.. There have been a lot of shootings and people killed in that area over the years, but nothing has changed. A police car has been parking with the lights on in front of the building twenty-four hours from time to time. But there is still a lot of shootings and violence going on in that neighborhood. She herself had been shot in the legs and her brother gunned down over there few years ago. She had also been jumped and beaten in her building few days before she came to see me at my place in Silver Spring. Her face was still bruised.

She got off the bed and called her daughter. "Guess where I am and with who?" she said on the phone with a large smile on her face. "I am with Leo" at his place. She told me before calling her daughter, that her daughter always asked her why she was not in a relationship with me, and that I was a very nice person.

I took her and her daughter to the movies when I first met her. And since then, I had helped them a lot over the three years I have known her.

The second time she came there, we had an argument about a mess she left on my living room carpet while emptying tobacco out of a cigar to use it as roll up, and never cleaned behind her, before she left in the morning. The first time she came there.

She denied it and started shouting that I was accusing her of being messy. She kept screaming that she was a clean person, and I was falsely accusing her of being messy. I had the whole mess recorded on my phone, but she still denied it, after I showed it to her and became more and more belligerent and louder. I called an Uber and told her I would talk to her another time, because I didn't want the shouting and screaming in my place. Since I moved there, I kept my place peaceful, and my neighbors never heard any noise coming from me. I rarely had visitors there. I liked to keep myself in a peaceful environment. I really did not like too much noise myself.

I had past experiences with dramatic relationships, and I am not looking to go back to that ever in my life. I love peace and happiness and harmony. I stay away from drama and chaos.

From the little time she and I spent together, I can tell that if we were into a serious relationship, we would not be compatible, intellectually, mentally, and psychologically.

I gave her a copy of my books years ago. I don't think she ever cared to read them. I would not want to be in a relationship with someone in whose company I will be bored and with whom I won't be able to enjoy having conversations on things that I am interested in, like politics, religion, culture and anything mentally stimulating.

I was not looking for any relationship that will be more drama than a positive interaction. I was not in a rush to find the right mate. My priority was to get myself in a more stable situation before getting involved into any serious relationship.

I was just helping her because I liked her as a buddy and because I love to help people anyway. A lot of older men out here are being targeted by younger ladies who may pretend to care about them but are only interested in getting money from them. I felt like that was what she thought she was doing with me.

"No, you not" I said back to tease her. I gave her enough money to get herself something at the Chinese carry out across the street.

She called me early on Thursday, November 26, 2020, Thanksgiving day, to ask me to buy her a disposable aluminum turkey roasting pan. She received a free turkey from a place that gives free turkey to poor families during thanksgiving and Christmas. She did not have any pan to bake it in. I told her to meet me at the Safeway on New York Avenue and 4th street. I got up from my friend's couch, took a shower and rode my bike to Safeway. I did not mind doing it so that she and her daughter could enjoy their thanksgiving day. Besides, the pan costs only a few dollars. I got at Safeway before she got there although she lives 3 blocks away. "Where are you? Look, I am leaving if you don't bring your ass up here in the next 5 minutes" I said to her on the phone angrily. I rode my bike for 15 minutes to get there, but she lives right around the corner but still had not got there before me. "I'm coming now, don't go nowhere" she said. She showed up with her daughter about 7 minutes later. I

TURNING MY NIGHTMARES INTO A BETTER DREAM

thought she only needed the pan, but she ended up asking me if she could get more stuff. Her daughter kept grabbing stuff and adding it to the cart. I ended up spending nearly $60, although I was expecting to spend no more than $20. I gave her and daughter $20 a piece in addition to what I spent. I headed downtown to start selling my books early on thanksgiving day.

I was happy I helped a poor mother and her daughter have a real thanksgiving meal, although nobody offered me one, except the strangers who were driving around and giving plates to the homeless. One such person parked by me while I was selling my books on the streets and offered me a plate. I was grateful.

One night, I was at my spot selling my books. It was around 8pm. I got a text message on my phone from my same lady friend. "Can you order a pizza for me and my daughter? We are hungry. We have no food in the house." Said the message. I started thinking. Here I am, a homeless living in a tent and this woman who has a place to live is constantly asking me to spend money and do things for her. Although I don't mind. I could understand if she had asked me to get her some groceries, so that she can have some food in her house for several days. But here she is asking me to order some pizza for her and her daughter. And she has the nerve to tell me where to order it from and what toppings she wanted on it.

I myself did not spend money on pizza. I was making money selling my books on the streets, but I was still a homeless man. I budgeted the little money I make and tried to spend as little and save as much as I could. I would not spend $20 on a pizza, when I could get more food for that same amount. I texted her back and told her that I was about to ride my bike back to my tent, and that the best I could do for her, and her daughter was to get her some frozen pizza at Safeway on my way to my tent. I could get her four large frozen pizzas for the same price as the large pizza that she wanted me to order.

I told her that I would get her some frozen pizza at Safeway, when I finish selling my books and head to my tent. I went to Safeway on New York Avenue and texted her to ask her what type of frozen pizza she wanted from there. They had some large pizza on sale. Two for $10.

She texted me back and listed more items she wanted. I told her that I would get the pizza and whatever else on the list that I could but would not spend more than $30. I didn't mind helping her and her daughter, but I was not going to spend on groceries for her, all the money I made that day.

I got her two large pizzas with the toppings that she wanted. I also got her some juice and other stuff that I cannot remember now. I left the store and called her to let her know that I was about to be in front of her building in two minutes with her stuff.

She asked me "what stuff?" I was surprised. She acted like she had no idea what I was talking about. I mentioned the texts that she sent me. She got silent for a minute. I guess she paused to read the texts. "I will meet you in front of the building" she told me. I got there. She came down and explained that she did not send the texts, but her daughter did that without her knowledge, and pretended to be her.

She apologized. Her daughter was 14 and pregnant at the time. I didn't know. I found that out when my friend told me few months later that her daughter just had a baby. I realized then that her daughter was really hungry because of the pregnancy and took it upon herself to text me from her mother's phone to try to get me to get her some food.

I have more stories of me helping a lot of homeless ladies and poor single mothers, but I will not share all of them here.

I know it makes no sense to be homeless on the street and use the money I make to help others who have a roof over their head, instead of putting all that money up to get my own place at the right time. But I did that because I just wanted to help others who were facing an urgent situation. I know, I am still not making sense no matter what explanation I may come with. I guess, I am just a nice person who cares about other people, I am not saying that to brag about what I do for others. I am just showing that I am not a selfish person, and I don't mind helping others when I can or feel compelled to.

My philosophy in life is that the more I give, the more I receive. I am not advising anyone to neglect their own needs and take care of others first. I am just saying that it is ok to help others while we are trying to improve our own reality. But, although that is how I feel about not being selfish, it is wise to make sure your urgent and important needs are met, and that you make progress in attaining your goals while helping others.

I know I could have told myself, Leo, you got your own problems. You can't help anybody until you help yourself. I do not necessarily disagree with that, but at the same time, I still think that I should not be selfish to the point of not helping anybody at all. I can still put most of what I make aside and use a tiny little bit to help others. I can use anywhere from 5% to 10% of what I make and help others with that, while using 90 to 95 percent to take care of myself and still accomplish my goal.

I was able to help others because I was doing very good with my street book selling. But I was not saving enough to get a place like I said. I even became inconsistent with my street book selling. I spent a lot of time in my tent playing chess on my phone and just relaxing instead of going out there to sell books.

I had started writing my second book but found myself spending hours and hours on my cell phone either playing chess or watching and commenting videos on YouTube or writing long posts on Facebook. I will admit that playing chess online on my phone became addictive.

When we think of addiction, we only think of substance abuse. But spending a lot of time on social media or playing games on cell phones is a problem that is comparable to drug addiction. What is even more detrimental with cell phone addiction is that it uses up too much of the time that we should use to make things happen.

We know that our time in this life form is limited and that one day we will die and be gone. But we tend to live as if we always have time to do what we are supposed to do but are not doing until a problem happens.

Chapter 3:
SURVIVING THROUGH CALAMITIES

(I learned how to survive and make the best out of the worse of situations)

In life, sometimes, we look at problems as the end of the world, despair sets in, and we give up on believing in our ability to overcome and make things better. But I came to the realization that I had the potential and abilities in me to come up with a way to survive through this new and unexpected challenge.

In 2020, Washington DC like the rest of America was shut down because of a pandemic caused by the Corona Virus. On March 30, of that year, Mayor Bowser declared a state of emergency for the District. I was totally caught off guard. I had no idea how I was going to make any money, since I could no longer sell my books on the street. I was less afraid about catching the virus and more concerned about how I was going to survive. I wondered what I would do, after the stay-at-home order was going to go into effect on April 1.

The order stated that: "Residents may only leave their residences to engage in essential activities, including obtaining medical care that cannot be provided through telehealth and obtaining food and essential household goods, to perform or access essential governmental functions, to work at essential businesses, to engage in essential travel and to engage in specific recreational activities that the order defined. Anyone found to be violating the order would be charged with a misdemeanor and subject to a $5,000 fine and/or 90 days in prison. (to be rephrased in my own words)."

I sincerely doubted that the police would arrest homeless people who had no home to stay in and would therefore be in violation of the stay away order. Nonetheless, I was in a total state of confusion. I was not so concerned about catching the virus, but I was more worried about how I was going to make any money to survive, since I could no longer go sell my books on the streets. The Pandemic was a perfect example of how I was able to see a problem as an opportunity to achieve something better than the predicament I was in.

I decided to use the internet and social media to sell my books, since I could no longer make any money on the streets. I got Brad to help me build a website. Brad is the one who took the picture that is on the cover of my book. He is a good Samaritan. I met him when he was looking for a homeless man to give him a jacket that he promised him, when he saw him earlier in the day but did not find him, when he came back with it to the place where they were supposed to meet. I named it homelesslivesmatterbook.com after my book, Homeless Lives Matter, Homeless My story. But the website alone was not enough to attract viewers. I thought about starting a Facebook page, but I ended up focusing on starting an Instagram page and building it. I named it homelesslivesmatterbook. I attracted followers and grew my audience fast by posting daily on how I was surviving through the pandemic every day.

I want to share few of the posts that I shared daily on my Instagram page, homelesslivesmatterbook, to document chronologically, how I survived during the covid pandemic shutdown.

May 2020

-Coronavirus outbreak is making life harder for the homeless because everything is shut down. But in my tent, I use my imagination to create a meal that is healthy but cheap and easy to make.

-My meal of the day. Avocado mixed with Tuna in oil, mayo, ketchup, hot sauce. And organic fruit spread mixed with peanut butter. And Ritz crackers ha ha. I am surviving the best I can in isolation.

-The Laundromat where I normally wash my clothes, has been shut down since the Coronavirus outbreak.

- I figured out that I could spread my larger tarp on the grass and capture some rainwater last week when it rained for a couple of days. Then use the rainwater to wash my clothes and dry them the next day when it was sunny.

SURVIVING THROUGH CALAMITIES

-The other day, two security officers came and told me that I could not be here. But hey, I am back again. I got to write. Public libraries are closed, because of covid 19. But I still got to write my next book. The hell with covid 19. It ain't gonna stop me from writing wherever I can find a place to keep my laptop charged.

I am feeling a little stressed. It is 7:24 pm. This is my meal for the entire day. Just two cans of tuna with mayo and some herbs and spices seasonings and some strawberry fruit spread on the side. And some mountain dew. I normally don't consume that much soda drink, but once in the blue moon. I am here in the woods, trying to survive the best I can until this Coronavirus nonsense go away and everything gets back to normal.

-My meal of the day. Tuna and mayo with some spices and crackers again. Yes, it is depressing to eat the same thing over and over and over again every day. But hey, it is healthy, and I will not starve during this pandemic shut down. I can survive on the tuna and crackers u till things get back to normal. I stay right here away from everybody, so I won't worry about catching Coronavirus. I can't afford to get sick. So, I am here in the woods (not totally) and surviving on the little food I got here. I am grateful.

-I am updating my website right now, outside here while charging my laptop. The security guards of the building ask me to leave several times in the past. But when you homeless and have no home to charge your stuff, hey they chase you, but you don't give up. Hope one day, I won't have to go through so much suffering and humiliation. But hey, that's life. I am grateful.

-Just took a hot shower at the Downtown Day Services Center for the homeless, located inside the New York Ave. Presbyterian Church at 1313 New York Ave. NW. I had to make a reservation on Tuesday to be able to take a shower today. I am glad they are still doing showers although on appointment even though they are not providing all the services as usual and only allowing inside the building, whoever has an appointment for shower or laundry.

-The days I got to wait till I can make it to a hot shower, I just go get a gallon or two of water at a corner store about 7 blocks down the street and shower right outside my tent. I don't care how cold the weather and the water are, I got to shower every day. Being homeless doesn't mean that you got to forget about your hygiene. No excuse not to clean your body every day. Sorry. I got to.

-Hey, I also had to wash my clothes. The Laundromat where I normally do my laundry is not open back yet cause of Coronavirus restrictions. Cause I am homeless doesn't mean I got to feel comfortable wearing dirty clothes. It is always a way, no matter what. We always got to try to find a solution to any issue we face. If I am not giving up. You shouldn't. Stay blessed, whoever you are.

-I stashed my little bucket, body wash, and lotion in these bushes. Wow, they are still there. About to take a quick shower outside here while the streets are still deserted. I had to ride 20 minutes down here to be able to shower outside here before I start my day. Need to be fresh to start a new day with a clear mind. No matter what you go through, stop complaining. No need to depress yourself. Just do what you got to do to feel

better.

-Blake and Sarah, two strangers I met on Instagram, cared enough to bring me 17 gallons of water and some packs of Tuna and crackers. I don't know how to thank them enough for taking their precious time and drive all the way up here to give water to a 55-year-old homeless man living in the bushes. I am so touched; I don't know what to say.

JUNE 2020

-I got soaked last night on my way back. Once here, I spread a tarp and captured rainwater. I am filtering it in a 3-gallon bottle and will add a bit of alcohol to disinfect and use it to clean up. I saved the rest for the future, so I won't use my drinking water for hygienic purposes. Always try to make the best of the situation even on a rainy day. Rainwater, free water. Use it.

-I am watering my tomato plants with rainwater I captured and saved a couple of days ago. Even a homeless person can grow food. All you need is a slice of tomato with grains in it and some soil. Water is free from the rain. Just figure a way to capture when it rains and save it in empty water bottles. Where there is a will there away.

-We are still in phase 1 opening here in DC (Coronavirus pandemic restrictions). If you have washing and drying machines in your house or your building, consider yourself blessed. It is people outside here who have to go through headaches to get their clothes washed. Enjoy your blessings

and don't complain about insignificant things. Somebody out here is doing worse than you. Don't worry. Be happy.

-I Spread a tarp on the ground to collect rainwater to use to shower. Homeless or not, no excuse, I still got to wash my behind. Free water from the sky. For every situation, there is a solution. Just take your time and figure it out. Survival is a must. Don't stress.

-I am riding my bike by this woman sleeping under scaffolds by an apartment housing construction site at 3:00 pm under 83-degree temperature.

-Laundromat closed earlier. Couldn't make it. Had to hand wash few clothes items to have some clean to wear till I get to laundry tomorrow. As I always remind all of you, there is always some kind of solution to a difficult situation. So don't let any problem stress you. Yes, I am in downtown Washington dc handwashing my clothes. So, what if somebody sees me? Can't let pride and shame get in the way.

-I stashed a laundry bag filled with dirty clothes and a bottle of Gain detergent in these bushes here in downtown Washington DC, till tomorrow when I am finally able to get to the laundromat up the street. I am not worried about anybody stealing my dirty clothes. If they do, then they must really need it. I won't be mad.

July 2020

-I Just took a nice shower outside my tent. Feeling fresh. About to go downtown ship few more books and take care of business. Forget my issues, worries, or problems. I got to stay *focused on turning this day into a productive day, by the time I get back here late in the night. If you have not ordered your book yet, what you waiting on? Come on, we all got to eat! Haha. Stay blessed.*

-I came to my friend's apartment for a night. I give him $20 for a night whenever I decide to come here to feel in a cool place and escape the heat in my tent.

-I want to express my gratitude to Laney for dropping a cooler, some ice, and some water by my tent a few minutes ago. Thank you so much to all of you who take some of your time to show compassion for the homeless. Thank you again, Laney (laneybogs08). Stay blessed

-I try to stay positive but sometimes situations can be overwhelming, but I am still ok. First, I just left the clinic to get checked for a lump in my chest above my heart, that has been bothering me for a week now. The doctor thinks it might be fibrosis. But she gave me a referral to get a mammogram. Hopefully, it is not cancer. When I stepped outside, my bike tire was gone. Somebody stole my bike wheel while my bike was locked right in front of the clinic. The security dude let me keep the bike inside the facility till tomorrow at 9:00 am cause I cannot carry the bike on the bus without the back tire. This was not a good day. But I am not gonna complain. Haha. Left laughed before I get too upset and shed tears. Can't afford to do that. Being 54 years old and going through so much hardship is not nice haha. But I am still alive. Something to be grateful for, I guess. Although it is a f-cked up life. I guess it is just bad luck. I will be ok.

-Before I left this morning, I opened the tent wide to let everything dry. I am back before the rain forecast for 7:00 pm starts. I made sure I checked the weather this morning and got back here in time. When I got back here last night after the storm, the floor of my tent was flooded. I emptied the water in a bucket and will use it to water my tomato plants. Surprisingly, my tent-top mattress was not soaked. I had a peaceful sleep.

 -When I came back the night before Yesterday, my tent was flooded. I did not look at the water on my tent floor as a problem. I collected it and fill a 7-gallon water jar plus another water gallon bottle and save all that water for my tomato and garlic plants. It had been really hot lately and the plants were dying until the storm breaks these last two days. But the heat may resume soon and at least I got water saved for the plant. Water may look dirty because dirt may have got in, but the plants will benefit from it. A lesson of the day, turn a problem into a solution, maybe not for you but someone else or an element of nature.

-Came to my buddy's place to take a long cold shower. On my way back to my tent before rain starts. Finding a place to take a shower can be a headache for the homeless, mostly for women out there.

-Got my tent covered this time. Rain started. The lesson of the day. Always be prepared mostly for predictable situations. If you don't then the calamity that comes your way will be self-inflicted. Learn that lesson from the last time when I did not check the weather forecast and left without covering my tent and came back to find the tent flooded.

August 2020

-It is 5:30 am. I feel very hungry. Just got some mocha, a can of tuna salad snack, and two bananas from 7/11. I woke up around 3:30 am to some noise outside my tent. When I peeped through the screen, I saw a pair of eyes shining in the dark outside towards me. I thought of either a cat or a raccoon. Most probably a raccoon. Anyway, when you sleep outside, you are subjected to be awakened constantly by all sorts of noises and the abrupt presence of animals or humans in your immediate surrounding.

-I was blessed by Yoojin and her friends. They just brought me a small table and a chair. Now I can write in my tent. I broke the chair I had and with no table and chairs, it is very hard to write inside a tent. I want to express my gratitude to Yoojin and her friends. Thank you so much

-It rained abundantly the previous couple of days. As some of you already know, I do collect rainwater as I am doing this morning and filter it and use it for personal hygiene or to water the tomatoes and garlic I am growing around here. I am not drinking it though. I could not make it to a shower place, so I have to shower out there. I wear long shorts that reaches my knees, so I won't be accused of indecent exposure, although no pedestrians are walking by and the cars on the road cannot see me because I am behind my tent. There is no human habitat or business around here. It is only nature and peace and quietness. So, I am not bothering anybody.

-I am about to go to sleep on somebody's couch tonight with a fan blowing right above my head in this old building with a ceiling fan barely blowing some air and with no air conditioner.

Though I prefer my bed in my tent to a couch, I am still grateful that my friend opens his doors to me to come inside anytime I feel the need to come inside. At least I can sleep tonight without hearing insects and birds making all sorts of noises all night, haha. Anyway. Hopefully, I wake up in the morning to see another day.

- Just waking up on somebody's couch. Kind of missing my bed in my tent. Sleeping on a couch gives me neck pains that I don't need now. Haha. But I am grateful that somebody opened their door to me for a night and in exchange, I could also help them with $20 that they can use since they are also poor.

-8:00 am. Riding my bike by this homeless man sleeping in the median lane during heavy morning traffic on one of Washington DC's busiest highways. Seems like homelessness is getting worse. Anybody paying attention?

-9:45pm. I had gone to my tent, a couple of hours ago. But because of the rain these couple of days, it seems like the whole area around my tent is infested with mosquitoes. It was a little stressful to have to deal with the humidity and mosquitoes. So, I called my friend and asked if I could come and sleep on his couch for tonight. He said yes. I made a stop at the Giant store and got myself some stuff to cook while I am here for the night. I got dishwashing soap since I know he had a little bottle the last time I was here and most likely he had run out. I gave him $20 as usual for a night.

-4:13 pm. I am walking by a cemetery and feeling like it is the place to rest in peace after suffering so much in this life. But no

rush, hahaha. We all gonna end up there. Until then, I can only try to feel ok even when feeling depressed.

-7:00pm. I just woke up in my tent after taking a nap when I came back from returning to my friend's place to pick up my solar charger that I forgot when I had come to my tent the first time this afternoon. When I return here and rest on my bed, I fell into a deeper and restful sleep than sleeping on a couch. Many homeless do not get appropriate sleep because they don't sleep on a comfortable bed. So, one thing I made sure of is to have brought a bed here in my tent. Although it is better to be indoors than outside, at least I got this bed here which makes sleeping out here more restful.

-10:10am. Left my tent at 8:00 am. Got to SOME and took a shower by 8:45 am. Now I am having breakfast (and most likely my only meal of the day) outside on a bench. Having fried croaker fish with fried eggs and home fries and bread a grape jelly and Iced tea lemonade mix. All for $10.20 from carry-out on New York and New Jersey Ave. in North West DC. My book is my source of income. It allows me to eat what I want.

-9:15 am. Another frustrating start today. I left SOME at around 8:50 am. I went there to take a shower. I left my tent at 8:20 am. I got to SOME at 8:32 am. I was the only one standing outside at the door for a shower. On the door, the sign says "Men showers from 6:00 am to 9:30 am and women Showers from 9:45 to 11:30 am.

-I decided to let the gentleman doing the showers know that I was waiting. I opened the door and saw him talking in the dining

room with other workers. I waited till he stepped out of the dining room and told him that I was waiting to take shower. He told me that the two homeless in showers were the last ones for the day. I closed the door and asked a lady outside what time it was. She told me 8:42 am. I opened the door back and asked another worker to call the supervisor for me. The gentleman steps back from the showers area as the lady supervisor walked towards the door. The gentleman stood right behind her. I asked to talk to her alone. He responded, "you gonna talk about me, so I want to hear". I asked to talk to her in private. She asked me to meet her in front of the building. I did but she never came. I returned to the entrance door. The gentleman stood there. I told him, I just want to make suggestions to her for some changes in the way this shower thing is run because it is so frustrating to come there at 8:38 am and be told that the shower is done for the day when the sign says showers end at 9:30 am. Then he changed the story. "you came here at 8:45 am and I told you that you might not be able to make it to the showers", he said. I told him that I talked to him at 8:38 am and he told me showers closed for the day after those in there come out. I got on my bike and left.

-The real issue here is that the gentleman is lazy and doesn't care about the homeless waiting to take shower. He normally sits at his desk and spends the entire time on his cellphone instead of monitoring the time each person spent in the shower so that the next person waiting can get in. Then he rushes to close the shower early. And he never clean showers after last used, for the next person. Things like that frustrate and discourage many homeless people from taking showers at places offering service to the homeless.

-1:30pm. I am back in my tent downtown. About to eat this meal that this lady cooked for me. Every Sunday, she fixes me a meal and I go pick it up by the senior citizen building where she lives. She is one of my angels. At least I know, every Sunday someone cares to make sure I got a home-cooked meal.

September 2020

-6:35 pm. I Just got to my tent. I am being attacked by millions of Mosquitos. It rained for the last couple of days that I was away. And I am being bitten left and right. They just invaded the whole area cause it is still wet. I think I am going back to my friend's place in North East.

-8:15pm. I came by Safeway to meet albaptist08 who brought me some comforter and pillows after I posted earlier about going to Forman Mills to get some blanket. Now, I don't need to worry about purchasing a blanket. It is a bit chilly outside here and I am getting on the bus to head to my tent. Thank you so much to Alex and all the angels out here who care for the homeless.

-10:20pm. I am in some downtown Washington DC back alley loading dock, charging my phone before heading to my tent for the night. Another homeless man sleeping in the doorway.

-11:00am. I am just waking up and about to take a cold shower outside my tent. It was chilly throughout the night. The cover I received from albaptiste08 kept me warm. Thank you again, Alex. You are an angel.

-4:46 pm. I am checking on some of the tomatoes I planted a few months ago around me as an experiment when the coronavirus epidemic started, and everything got shut down. I had planned to grow food in the woods in case things had got worse and food scarce. When toilet paper, then water, then bread shelves started getting empty as stores, O had to think of plan B in case the shortages had extended to major food items, and everybody started looking for food. Haha. Homelessness has tough me a lot about survival. You got to think ahead instead of panicking when uncertainty shows on the horizon. That is one of the things I am writing about in my next book.

October 2020

-4:30 pm. Another Angel, by the name of Faith, found a bike for me from her circle of bike riders. She asked around if someone had a free bike, and here we. She drove her hour away to bring me this bike. I am so amazed and humbled by the kindness and support I am getting from many of you reading my posts here. Thank you, a lot Faith, for this bike. It will help a great deal during this period of the coronavirus pandemic. At least I don't have to worry about public transportation. A bike will take me anywhere. I am grateful.

-12:06 PM. After sleeping on someone's couch for a week in order so that I could be indoors, away from mosquitoes, I am finally back in my bed. But my bed outside, in a tent of course. More comfortable than a couch, though. But sleeping on somebody's couch inside a house is preferable to doing so on a comfortable bed outside. I am not trying to glamorize the

homeless by any means. But I can sleep and see something enjoyable in every situation, good or bad. So, I am gonna enjoy this bed and not the fact that it bothers me because it is outside. I am grateful.

I am Charging my portable power with my solar charger right by the tent in nature. One of the Angels who have supported and helping for a long time, got it for me when the pandemic started so that I could be safe and not worry about coming downtown to charge my phone. I receive so many blessings from total strangers and I am grateful for that. I also feel it as a duty to use the extra I get to also help those around me in dire need, whenever I can.

-Me fooling around with this praying mantis climbing on my bike. I just love observing these beautiful little creatures in this natural environment, which they don't mind sharing with a homeless man. We need to stop destroying the environment, which is their natural habitat, otherwise, these beautiful creatures will become extinct.

-Haha. Sometimes, I feel safer around animals, wildlife, trees, and plants. Human beings are the most dangerous creatures on this planet. This is why we all need to contribute to increasing compassion, empathy, and respect for our fellow humans.

November 2020

-12:00am. Stopping by the cemetery on my way back to my

friend's place. I believe that I am on this earth for a purpose and that I am not gonna be here forever. So, stopping by a graveyard helps me appreciate life even in the predicament I am and understand that time is pretty short.

-I am here with the crowd at the White House today Saturday, November 7, 2020, witnessing history taking its course. The first woman elected Vice-president of the United States. I also came across this homeless brother. Not a Trump supporter. I don't agree with his choice of some of the words he used to refer to Trump. But those words are street vernacular. But today, after a long depressing wait, a winner was declared by the media. some are happy, others are not. This is Democracy. Somebody wins, somebody loses. But life goes on. We still got to love one another.

-5:50pm. I got the tent set back up. I didn't nail it to the ground very tight the last time I left. I will be back tomorrow morning to take everything out and mostly the mattresses and let them dry all day. I might have to spend tomorrow night on my friend's couch because I need to let the inside of the tent dry out. Some rain got into it. But that's my fault. I didn't plan to be gone for so long

-I came to pick my Thanksgiving dinner from Yesterday. This will also be my birthday dinner. This nice lady that I have known from her from Franklin Park in NW Washington DC, where they use to feed and hand out hygiene stuff and clothes the Homeless. Her name is Arlene. When the Coronavirus pandemic shut everything down, I could no longer make money selling copies of my book, Homeless Lives Matter, Homeless

My Story, on the street. Though I had lost touch with her, she reached to me to check on me and offered to cook a homemade meal for me every Sunday. The last Sunday, I met her, she told me she was gonna have a Thanksgiving dinner for me. When she called Yesterday, I slept in the day after I spent nearly 24 sleepless hours getting book orders ready. So, I did not have Thanksgiving dinner Yesterday. I am about to enjoy this meal prepared by this angel. I feel so blessed to have all these angels around me. I believe that angels are a real human being that shows up on your path at the right time to bless you unexpectedly. I am so great that despite all the miserable experiences I have been having, there are still great human beings out there who can empathize without casting judgment.

-5:03pm. I am outside on a bench by the bushes where I stash my dirty clothes until I take them to laundry nearby. I decided to spend my birthday outside so that I can remind myself that I am still homeless, although I have been able to go indoors and sleep on my friend's couch or floor for a couple of weeks. I will be heading to my tent to meditate and reflect on my journey so far. Seems like I am seeing some light at the end of the tunnel, but I am still conscious of my current homeless situation while working hard to end it permanently. I have been homeless off-on for a long time. But now, with my writings, doors are opening. I am grateful. I am not complaining. This meal is delicious, blessed be the sister who prepared it out of compassion and pure kindness. Leo

December 2020

-2:00pm. I made my appointment with the dentist at SOME dental clinic for the homeless. Time for dentures. Last year, I had about 10 teeth pulled. I was in the process of getting dentures when the Coronavirus pandemic shut everything down. So, I am getting back with the process and hopefully, I will be able to properly chew again and eat some of the food I like but can't eat now. I am glad I can my book and buy my own food so that I won't rely on food from soup kitchens that may not be able to properly digest. I am grateful. While at the same time, I want to let you know that dental care although available for the homeless in Washington DC, is still a concern. Hopefully more homeless have access to dental care. And I am grateful for places like SOME dental clinic here in Washington DC. They doing a good job.

February 2021

-The air outside is so fresh and pure. I feel like in heaven walking outside in the snow. Tomorrow is another day. Hopefully, tomorrow will give birth to good news. Hopefully, I wake up to see tomorrow. We shouldn't take anything for granted in this life. Every second we are still here on this earth is something we should be grateful for.

-Some angel is willing to rent me an apartment. Thank you to everyone who supported me and my book. I have saved as much as I could so I would no longer have to sleep outside or on somebody's couch or floor. I am grateful to you all. Although it is not finalized yet, I am in the process of renting an apartment from a landlord, who is willing to rent to a homeless man who only relies on selling his book as an income. I call this a miracle.

-Tomorrow I am picking up keys for my apartment. I just signed the lease and will pick the keys tomorrow. There are fixtures to be made on Monday. But I will be working on getting some furniture this weekend. Landlord asked for the first month and security deposit. I went ahead and paid first and last month's rents plus security deposit, therefore 3 months of rent. The transition will not be easy because I have been a chronic homeless, meaning for more than 10 years (Off and on though). The trauma I endured for so long, of homelessness will not dissipate overnight.

-5:00pm. Sleeping in my own bed, in my own place is so therapeutic. I feel like I am in a hospital recuperating. Wow, my whole body and mind are feeling the effect of real rest and relief and healing.

-11:45 am. I woke up a couple of hours ago in a place where I can call my own as long as I pay my rent every month. I have been a chronic homeless off and on for so long that I am ashamed to say. For the last 3 months, I slept on my friend's couch and floor. But for a little over 5 years, I lived in a tent that I set up in a wooded area, away from everybody. I had so many nightmares, sometime back-to-back the same day, that I was scared to go back to sleep. Sometimes, I would dream that I was in a nice place but woke up back in a tent.

-When I used to go out by old Ebbitt's grill, on 25th and G North West, Washington dc, right around the corner to the White House, my goal was to save enough to get me a nice place. Although I could sell at least two books in an hour (I was selling my book for $10 a copy on the street), I was not able to save

enough to even think about trying to find a place to rent. But because of covid 19, I was forced to activate my website and focus on selling my book online. When on my birthday, I decided to do a fundraiser to get rid of 100 books I had stored at my friend's place, so many of you responded by ordering a bit over a thousand in 2 days November 22 and especially, November 23). Today it is because of the generosity, kindness, and support of all of you, that I am in a warm place of my own this morning while it is snowing this morning. I want to thank every single of you who have supported me, either by ordering a copy or simply donated. And I apologize to the few of you who did not get their copies yet for reasons that I have already explained and trying to correct so that there won't be future occurrences. I want you to know, I am so grateful to you. Thank you, one thousand times.

CHAPTER 4

I TURNED BAD LUCK INTO GOOD LUCK

(Create an opportunity for yourself even in the midst of calamity)

I was finally seeing the light at the end of the tunnel. I had made enough money to afford a place. But because I had been homeless for so long and did not have a recent rental history or a regular job, it was still going to be difficult to convince any landlord to just trust me and rent to me. I decided to put an ad in craigslist, instead of applying to regular rental companies. I thought I had a greater chance of getting a place from a private landlord if, I could convince him or her that I had enough money to cover a year worth of rent. I went ahead and put the following ad up on craigslist.

Homeless activist author seeking an apartment or basement to rent

I am looking for an apartment or a basement to rent for less than $1500 or less. I am currently homeless but staying with a friend. I am an author and I have $10,000 saved towards finding a place to rent. But because I have lived in a tent for so long as homeless, I have no rental history. Whoever rent me their apartment or basement will not have any problem with their rent money. I am a 55-year-old and very peaceful and quiet and am seeking to be in a peaceful and quiet environment to write. I am currently sleeping on my friend's couch, and I need to move in my own place because I am not proper rest not having my own place which I can now afford. I am selling a lot of my books on my website and my social media pages. All I need now is a place to live. I saved enough money to do that. All I need is, find a renter to trust me to rent his apartment or basement and he/she will be happy he/she did.

I received an answer from a lady. She told me that she was visiting with her daughter in Virginia and that, in the few following days, she would return to Florida where she resided with her husband, half of the year during the winter. She was over sixty years of age. She told me that she had a two-bedroom apartment in a house in northern Silver spring that she was renting for $1300 a month, plus deposit. The place was half furnished, she wrote. I called her right away. She told me that her former husband was a pastor, and they used to help the homeless. I don't remember whether she meant feeding the homeless or any other type of service. But she showed empathy and asked me if I wanted to move in right away. I told her that I would come and visit the place and most likely move in right, after I decide that the place is ideal for me. She gave me the number of a tenant of hers who was residing in the basement and asked me to call her, so that she could show me the place. I asked her for the address. She told that me she would give it me when I was ready to go see the unit. I find it weird that she would not give me the address of the place that she agreed to let me rent, until I was ready to be on my way there. I wanted to know where the place was located and check on google map, what stores and amenities were in the vicinity. I thought she was a bit strange, but I had no doubt that she was a good person.

The next day, I called and told her that I was about to go check out the apartment. She gave me the address on the phone. I called an acquaintance who gave me a ride there. The place was located on a side street off Briggs Chaney Road, in the north easter part of Silver Spring. Silver Spring is located in southern Maryland and is part of Greater Washington DC, also known as the DMV (District of Columbia, Maryland, Virginia). The house was on a vast property that was unkept, at first sight from the front entrance. It was in the winter. The trees were leafless, and the yard had little vegetation on it. The parking lot looked like a junkyard with several vehicles with no tags, a van and couple of trailers. A couple of boats were visible on the other side of the house. I got a bit confused when I looked at the house. There was the main house and another dwelling on top of the house. I called the lady who was living in the basement. She was obese, tall and had a cane. We greeted her and entered the front part. She was standing on the steps leading to her unit in the basement. The unit she was about to show me was on the top of the stairs. She walked laboriously to the front door of the main unit of the house, opened it and invited us inside. The place looked like in the picture. I loved it. But the carpet was disgusting to look at. It was green and had a strong stench of dog and cat urine. My first thought was to get rid of that carpet before moving in. I was born with severe asthma, but I outgrew it when I was around 17 years of age. I have an allergy to cat hair. When I am exposed to it, I instantly develop asthma like attacks, mainly shortness of breath and chess tightness. I cannot therefore live in a place full of cat hair.

I told the tenant who was the showing me the place that I liked it. She told me to call the landlady and let her know. I did. I returned to DC to my friend where I was staying. I was supposed to meet the landlady at the house the next day to sign the lease. But I received a text from her to tell me that she and her husband had left the area and flew back to Florida earlier to avoid getting in the snow storm that was about to start. She emailed me a lease form a day later. I filled it, signed it and emailed it back. I told her that I was going to change the carpet at my own cost. She had no problem with that. She asked me if I wanted to keep the few pieces of furniture that was left there by the previous tenant. There were a couch, some chairs, a dining table, and few other pieces of furniture. They looked old. I did not want any of them. I told her that I would buy my own furniture and bring it in. She asked me to keep the furniture in my second bedroom until she comes back in the area from Florida in the Spring. We were in January. I was moving in on February 1st, 2021. I didn't mind keeping her stuff in my second bedroom for a couple of months, although I needed the space in there to stock my books and shipping supplies. April came and I did not see her or hear from her. She only sent me an email at the end of every month to let me know how much I owed for utilities for the previous month. In May, she texted me that she will be back in the area from Florida and will come move her stuff from the second bedroom. At the end of May she sent me an email about how much I owed for utilities for May. She did not say anything about when she would come and get her stuff from my second bedroom. I had a lot of boxes of books and envelopes crammed in my living room and was running out of space. In June, I noticed a chubby old man mowing the lawn. I assumed that he was probably her husband,

and that she was back in town and would soon call or text me to come and meet me for the first time and get her stuff out of my second bedroom. But I did not hear from her. I saw a big lady in the backyard one day with the old man, plus the other tenant who was renting a two-bedroom apartment located above the garage. I assumed that she was my landlord. I really could not understand why she was not coming to meet me, at least. I had been renting from her and sending her my rent, plus utilities money faithfully for four months. I felt cheated because I was paying $1300 for rent for a two-bedroom apartment, but I could not use my second bedroom. It had become a storage for the furniture of my landlord.

I started messaging her about the room. I needed that room; I was paying for it. She kept messaging me to apologize and promise that she will come and get the stuff out of there, but she never followed suit. One night, I came home from downtown DC. As soon as I entered the front of the house and walked the stairs to my unit, I smelled a foul smell coming from the vents. It was even worse when I entered my unit. The smell was coming from the vents in the floor of each room. I tried to ignore the smell, but it was getting stronger every day. It smelled like some wet carpet or some mildew or some sewage. I texted her to let her know. She told me that a unit in the basement had some flooding, and she was going to have someone come to fix the problem. She texted me later to tell me that someone will come and check my unit for any leak. That was the first time I met her.

She came and knocked on my door and apologized for having not come and meet me, all that time that she was back in the area from Florida. She was living on the premises all that time since she returned four months earlier. I was seeing her in the backyard from my window so many times. She told me that she would come with her 80-year-old husband to move some of the stuff to the other tenant's apartment and the rest to a trailer that was on the property. She did come with her husband two weeks later and I helped her move the stuff out of the room. So, I signed a one-year lease for a two-bedroom apartment but went 5 months without being able to use the second room. That was not fair. In addition to that, she had told me that all tenants in the house had to share the cost of utilities, but I later come to realize that I was the only one paying the utility bills which included water, electric and gas bills as well as cable and internet. She never showed me the bills but just gave me seemingly made-up numbers that kept increasing. I was paying anywhere between $250 to $340 per month for utilities. I lived by myself and did not consume that much electricity, gas and water. It was obvious to me that she was making me pay for the utility bill for the whole house. I knew she was taking advantage of me, but I was just grateful to have a roof over my head after having been homeless for so long.

There was an old washing machine and an old dryer in a room that separated my apartment from the apartment above the garage. The room was also used as laundry room. The tenant in that apartment had two cats. One of the cat used to belong to the tenants who moved out of my unit. The cat used to come and scratch my door, as if he wanted to return to the place that used to be its home. Although I like cats, because I consider myself a big cat, my allergies to their hair make it impossible for me to come close to them or to anything that has their hair on it. It was therefore a bit of an issue for me to get into that room to get my mail. I never had any allergic reactions from getting in there, grabbing my mail and snicking back into my apartment. I never used the washing and drying machines in that room. I did my laundry at a laundromat that was located in a small shopping center not far from the house.

Notalgia Paresthetica In My Back And Undiagnosed Mass In My Chest

Now that I had a place, I felt more comfortable going to the doctor and get checked for some of the health concerns that I dealt with for a long time, when I was homeless. The most urgent one was a sharp stabbing like pain in the upper left side of my back. I had that problem for seven or eight years now. The pain happens sporadically with a different frequency. Sometimes, it occurred once, or three times or ten times in a day or a week. It feels like someone is pushing a sharp nail or knife in my back. Sometimes, I caught myself screaming. The good thing is that the pain lasts only for a second or two and ceases. But I always feel the pain at the same precise spot. The area around the spot is burning and itching all the time, even now as I am typing this. It never stops burning. The itching can be intense sometimes. When I look in the mirror with my back facing the mirror, I see a dark patch of rash darker than my regular skin tone. I showed it to different doctors, on different occasions when I went to a clinic for something else. But none of them could tell me exactly what it was. During the coronavirus pandemic shutdown, I did not go to the clinic and hospital to get it checked, even though the pain was getting more frequent and more severe. I knew it was an urgency, but I didn't want to go to any hospital, because I didn't want to be exposed to the coronavirus. The news gave the impression that hundreds of thousands of people were dying from the pandemic. I thought hospitals were not a safe place to be, because too many patients with the virus were going there to get texted or treated. The virus is airborne. Which means that a patient with a face mask on, who touches anything in the hospital could infect the area and any object or wall in there. I waited until the pandemic subsided before I decided to get my doctor at the clinic to have a dermatologist look at it. I thought the skin rash was some kind of skin disease. I made an appointment with my doctor. But the visit was to take place via video conference. My doctor prescribed a supply of 6 months of Metformin pills for my diabetes. She also scheduled an appointment with the dermatologist and another appointment with a cancerologist at Howard university. The reason why she wanted me to go see that cancer specialist at Howard University was because I also had some concerns about a lump in my chest in my breast area. It was the size of a lime at first and then grew to the size of a lemon. It was not painful, but I could grab and move it. That mass in my breast caused me anxiety. But I was relieved when the doctors who checked me at Howard University, when I went to the appointment, concluded that it was something benign and not serious. They still wanted me to have a radiology test. I never did. It's been 2 years since, but I have not noticed any growth and have not had any pain in my breast.

I digressed a little bit. I was initially talking about the issue in my back. The dermatologist called me, and we had an appointment to meet through video conference. I missed her video call. But we still had a conversation on the phone when I returned her call. When I described the spot on my back and responded to few of her questions, she uttered" I know what it is, Notalgia Paresthetica. I had no clue what it meant.

According to the American Osteopathic College of Dermatology website, "Notalgia Paresthetica is a common condition that predominately affects adults. The main symptom is intense itching, burning, or a tingly feeling present along the inner part of the shoulder blade and the spine. Because of the constant rubbing in this area most patients develop a colored patch.

The most common cause of this condition in adults is pressure on a nerve root that gives sensation to the area."

She explained that I most likely had a problem with my spine. She scheduled me to a specialist to check my spine. I was relieved that it was not eczema or even shingles, as one doctor that I had seen for something else long ago, suggested.

The spine specialist who did some exams on my back, confirmed that I had a distorted spine that is putting pressure on the muscle on the left upper side of my back. The stabbing pain according to her, was caused by a nerve entrapped under the pressure of the muscle. She then had me see a chiropractor at the same facility. I made an appointment and returned to see him. He had me lie on my stomach while he performed some pressure on my spine. I heard a loud crack, as if someone had just broken some bones in my body. I screamed. It was painful. He told me that he had put back in place the distorted part of the spine. He assured me that I should no longer have the pain from the nerve in my back. I went back home and stayed in bed for two straight days. My back was hurting very bad in the area where he put pressure on my spine. This was a lasting pain in my entire middle back. But, after a good week, the pain was gone. I also did no longer had nerve pain for a while. But, after few months, the nerve pain was back but not as acute and frequent as before. No matter what health concerns I have been dealing with, my reality was better because I had a place and was not homeless anymore.

I got diagnosed with type two diabetes

I loved the place and was ok there. It was a very peaceful and quiet environment for the most part. I was to work on my second book, now that I had a place where I could relax and chill.

The pandemic had just ended but people were still socially distancing themselves from others. I could not go and sell my books on the street to pay my rent while taking my time to write the second book. And also, I had already sold a lot of copies of my first book online. I needed to come up with the second book as soon as possible so that I wouldn't run out of means to keep my place. I wanted the book to be inspirational and motivational. I was getting a lot of feedbacks and messages from folks following me on social media. They were getting inspired and motivated by my story and progress, from living in a tent to moving in my own place.

I wanted it published the sooner possible. I was on my laptop day and night writing and not getting the proper rest. My vision started getting blurry.

It seems like my vision deteriorating minute by minute. My mouth was staying dry, and I was thirsty all the time. I was constantly running to the bathroom to urinate.

I realized that something was wrong with me and that I needed to go the clinic urgently to get checked, but I kept procrastinating because I wanted to finish the book first.

I panicked and rushed to the clinic the following morning when I could no longer see clearly on the screen, what I was typing on the keyboard of my laptop or read anything on a piece of paper. They drew some blood and tested it. The doctor there told me that my blood sugar level was very high. He decided to give me a shot of insulin immediately and send me to the hospital emergency room right away. I got worried about that. I did not want to be shot with insulin. I have an aversion for syringe needles being inserted in my skin. I also did not want to become dependent on insulin shots. I was sure there was some pills that he could give me to bring my blood sugar level down until I get to the emergency room. I was lucky. The nurse could not find the insulin in the clinic. I don't remember whether he did give me some pills or not. But he did some paper work and asked me if I wanted an ambulance to take me to the emergency room. I told him that I could go on my own to Washington Hospital center on the D8 bus, from the bus stop across the clinic. My tent was located not far from the back of the hospital, although I had a place by then and was no longer living in the tent. I was so upset and very thirsty. I walked to the CVS store by the Rhode Island Metro station, bought a bottle of water and drank half of it at once. I walked to the station and caught a D8 bus heading to Washington Hospital Center. I got there around 7pm and checked in at the Emergency Room. I waited in a room with other patients for hours. A nurse had me taking IV fluids while waiting. A nurse came and got me around 12 am and sat me in a room by myself. She drew some blood and asked me about the reasons why I came to the Emergency Room. I looked at her and had no idea what to tell her. I was very confused and disoriented. I could not understand why I could not remember why I came to the hospital. She patted me on my tight and said" I understand". I am glad, I went to the clinic and was sent to the hospital emergency room from there. My blood sugar level at the clinic was 475. The normal level is between 70 to 100. Anything above 100 is above normal. My blood sugar level was way above normal. I probably could have ended into a diabetic coma, if I had stayed home and did not come to the clinic and hospital on time. The Doctor at the Emergency Room confirmed that I had type 2 Diabetes. He only prescribed me some Metformin 800 pills, plus some other medication, also pills. He told me that I did not need to be put on insulin. He also made an appointment with the ophthalmologist at the Washington Hospital Center eye clinic. I went there few days later and had my eyes checked. The eye Doctor told me that my blurry vision because of swelling of my pupils caused by high level of sugar in my blood. He also said that I did not have diabetes in my eyes. I don't know what that meant but I felt relieved. He told me to get some reading glasses until the swelling comes down, then I had to come back to have some glasses prescribed to me.

I was very sad and disappointed to have become diabetic. The doctor that I saw I the clinic a couple of weeks later, told me that I could reverse the Type 2 Diabetes, if I observe a strict low carb diet and lose weight. I was weighing around 270 pounds. This means no more ice cream, juices, sodas, pastries and sugary and starchy food. I also was prescribed some blood sugar or glucose monitoring device. It was hard for me to stick myself with anything that looks like a needle. But I had to do it to get some blood off my fingers to check my sugar or glucose level. I was able to do it once I did it the first time.

It seems like more and more men and women my age are contracting type 2 Diabetes. I am not surprised. Everything we eat has either sugar or salt in there. The Sodas, juices, cookies, cakes, and ice cream that we consume daily are poisoning us. I used to drink a lot of juices and sodas. Now I am paying a higher cost for pouring all that sugar in me.

My own home remedy for my Type 2 Diabetes

Although I took the medication that the Doctor prescribed, I also decided to explore natural remedies to reduce the sugar in my blood. Today, we can research anything online with a simple google search. I look up plants, fruits, roots, leaves, tree barks that have some medicinal properties capable of reducing blood sugar level. I went to an international store around where I reside and purchased some limes, about 20 of them, moringa leaves and seeds, mango leaves, and cinnamon sticks. I came back home, peeled the limes, added them in the blender with the other ingredients and blended everything. I drained it into a drainer, poured the concoction into a plastic jar and put it in the fridge. I wanted to do an experiment and see if it worked. I checked my blood sugar, took my diabetic medicine, and ate a meal right away. I waited about two hours later and checked my blood sugar level again. I had an idea of what my blood sugar level after taking my medicine. Then the next day, I checked my blood without taking the medicine. I had a meal and checked my blood sugar two hours after the meal. I figured out the difference in my blood sugar level when I took the medicine, Metformin and when I didn't, after a meal. I then drunk the concoction when I checked my blood sugar after a meal without taking my medicine. When I checked my blood sugar again, the result was perfect. My blood sugar was around 80. I purposely stopped taking the medicine and only drunk the drink I made. The result was always great. I am not advising anyone to stop taking their prescription and try what I did. Everybody body and organs react differently to different mixtures of natural elements. Some people may have an allergic reaction to what I made. But I know for sure that lime or lemon works pretty well on reducing blood sugar level. I am saying this because one day, I bought a pure 100 percent lemon juice, with no sugar added. I checked my blood sugar after I had it after a meal. The result was great.

I have seen too many homeless amputees in wheelchairs who had their legs cut off because of diabetic complications. I did not want to end up in a wheelchair with a foot or leg amputated.

So, I took this new problem very seriously. I survived homelessness for a long time and never had any major health issue. So, now that I had a place, it was important to take better care of my health since I was now able to cook my own meal and store fresh and healthy food.

When I was in the tent, I use to store my food in a cooler. I came in one day and noticed that some rats or mice entered the tent and chewed on the cooler. They got inside it and munched on the crackers.

Having a place of my own was such a relief. I was able to cook my own meal and no longer be limited as a homeless, about what food to eat or store or be able to prepare.

They Took All My Teeth Out And Left A Piece Of Bone In My Gum

I already had some dental issues before I got attacked near the homeless camp in the park on 9th and K street, North West. I actually had top and bottom partial dentures made in 2019, but I never wore them after I tried them at the dentist office and brought them home. I had paid about $900 out of pocket for them. I ended up removing them from my mouth, no more than a minute after wearing them in the house to see if I could get used to them. They were very uncomfortable in my mouth. I knew I should have taken them back to the dentist to get them adjusted. But I was frustrated because I knew that the dentist would try to convince me again to remove the three bottom incisors left in my mouth. The incisors are the four teeth in the front, at bottom and top of the mouth, between the two canine teeth on the bottom and top jaws. I still had my left and right canine left at the bottom. All the other teeth on my bottom jaw were missing. I also only had two molars, one at both ends, one left canine and one right pre molar left on my top jaw. Do the math to know how many teeth I had left in my mouth. You can imagine how hard it was for me to chew properly without any molar teeth at the bottom. Molars are the big teeth in the back of the jaws. Pre molars are the teeth after the molars. Then there is one canine tooth after the premolars. The incisive teeth are the four front teeth between the two canines.

I decided to get a denture after I had some tooth pain and needed to pull out the tooth that was causing the pain. I had cavities in three or four other teeth and few more damaged. The dentist wanted to remove nearly all the teeth remaining in my mouth, including all the bottom teeth, so that both top and bottom partial dentures would match and fit. But I wanted to keep in my mouth any tooth that was not damaged and was still solidly attached to my jaw. I ended up having 6 or teeth pulled in a couple of months in 2021 a month after I got off homelessness and moved into my place.

I was always embarrassed to open my mouth in public and conversed with people, because I was missing most of my teeth and particularly, my top front teeth. Many a times, some of the folks who read my posts on social media, invited me to speak in front of an online, but I either ignored their invitation or simply gave an excuses for the reason why I could not do it. I will admit that my esteem was kind of low when it comes to approaching women that I was interested in. I sincerely looked forward to getting the dentures so that I could masticate my food better and also feel unembarrassed to open my mouth and talk to people. I felt discouraged when I felt that the dentures were not comfortable. I just did not wear them. I decided that I would go to another dentist and make other dentures that I like better when I have enough money to do that. I had no problem with my dentist at SOME dental clinic, but I just did not like the dentures that was made there. She was such a nice doctor that I did not want her to feel like I did not like her work. So, I was contemplating having new dentures made by another dentist whose services that I could afford.

A year had passed since I had the dentures but never wore them. I was anxious to get new dentures so I could smile, eat properly and speak with people without feeling ashamed of having missing teeth in my mouth. But I never acted on it until the incident happened. The young men who attacked me by the homeless camp on 9th and K street, broke my top canine tooth and shook two of the three incisive teeth left on my bottom jaw. My bottom lip was wounded, and my mouth was in pain. I went to the dentist the next day. She gave me some antibiotics and some painkiller and reschedule me for an appointment in two weeks so that my mouth could heal before she does anything. I went back the day of my appointment. She removed three of the four teeth injured and had a male dentist remove the bone part of the canine that was left in my jaw since the top part was broken. The bone was solidly rooted. The dentist had a hard time removing it. I felt a strong pressure on my whole cranium as if a bone was being pulled out of my head. The dentist use a lot of force while trying to pull the tooth out. He seemed frustrated because he had a hard time getting a good grip on the teeth bone. All his attempts to pull it were unfruitful. He paused for a second and started cutting into my gums around the tooth. I did not feel any pain though since my mouth was numb. Nonetheless, I was a bit panicked because I felt like he was damaging my gum. But I kept my composure. He finally removed the tooth and stitched my gum. I went home and was in pain for I don't know how long. I could not eat anything solid for about a week. The gum healed faster than I expected. One of the complications of diabetes is that when a diabetic wound himself, the wounds takes longer to heal. But it was not the case with me. The only problem I had was that, about a week later, I kept feeling some cut into my upper lip anytime my lip came into contact with the stitched part of my upper gum. When I felt the area with my finger, I felt a sharp glass-like piece inside it.

I went back to the dental clinic the next morning. The dentist told me that there was a piece of broken bone that was stuck into my gum. She removed it. That piece was broken from my bone when the male dentist removed the piece of the broken tooth. It took me about a week before I totally healed. In the meantime, I could not eat properly all that time. I consumed mostly fluid. As a result, I lost a lot of weight within a couple of days. A couple more weeks later, I went back to the dentist to start the process of getting new dentures. I am wearing the dentures today. They are much better and more comfortable than the first ones that were made a year before. The only issue is that I am not able to eat with them. I tried, but it is not working. The bottom denture comes off. One day, when I make a lot of money, I will get some dental implants. But for now, all the little money that I make is for my rent so that I can keep a roof over my head and never be homeless again. That is my priority for now.

CHAPTER 5

I GOT OUT OF HOMELESSNESS BY WORKING FOR MYSELF

How did I get myself out of homelessness? The answer is simple: By working for myself. The first thing I hear people tell the homeless is "why don't you go get a job? To me, there are some homeless people who can do better as self-employed and through entrepreneurship. That is what I did, and it worked for me because I put in work.

I made of writing and selling my books, my profession, my occupation, and my main source of income as a self-published activist author. My work consists primarily of writing books, processing orders on my website, packaging, shipping, and selling them on the streets and online; and working on my social media platforms to grow my audience, advertise my books and attract more customers. This is a 24-hour 7-day work for me. I have been doing this alone most of the time. I rarely had someone help me. I can't afford to pay anybody at this stage. I am just making enough money to keep a roof over my head.

I finally was able to make and save enough money by working for myself and get out of homelessness. But now, the greatest challenge was how to keep being able to pay rent, keep a roof over my head and not be back into homelessness. That means that I had to sell at least 200 copies of my books monthly.

In November of last year (2022), I did a fundraiser to raise enough money to secure rent for the rest of the coming winter, so that I could rest during the winter and not worry about going outside to sell books on the street for rent. I even came up with the idea of having some customed-made inspirational baseball caps. I used a quote from my second book Survival And Life, The Lessons I learned. The quote in front of the hat says" Always Remember That You Are A Wonderful Being.". I wanted to have a large variety of colors because I really did not know what colors would be more popular. I did not want to have a limited choice of colors that could make my hats less attractive. I was very surprised that the colors that I thought were going to sell more, did not. The Red and Purple hats for example did not do to well contrary to my expectations. In life sometimes, we have to be prepared to make some adjustments when what we expect don't go according to our wishes. The hats did very well online. I was able to raise the money I needed for 4 months of rent ahead.

But I messed up several times when processing orders. I was working too hard by myself and not getting enough rest. I mistakenly shipped the same orders of books and hats multiple times to folks who already received their orders. It was a lot of money lost, but I still came out ok, although my profit margin was very slim. I decided not to charge for shipping cost, although it cost me a bit over $5 to ship a single book or hat order.

Many of my readers sent me donations, which helped offset the loss from shipping same order multiple times.

I spent entire days and nights processing and packaging orders and took them to the post office to be shipped. Sometimes, I went to different post offices to ship a few packages at a times, at each of them. I had a small, wheeled grocery cart tied to the back of my bike. I loaded it with packages, rode to the bus stop, put my bike on front of the bus and took the cart with me on the bus, got off the bus in downtown Silver Spring, tied the cart back to the bike and rode to the post office on Thayer Street. The two young black ladies at that post office were very kind and very professional all the time I went there. Neither of them ever complained about how many packages I had. I brought up to 30 at a time to the counter and they just processed them without any problem. I wanted to express my gratitude to them. So last Christmas, I offered each of them two of my Always Remember That You Are A Wonderful Being. I brought about 7 hats of different colors that I inserted in a Ziploc bag and had them pick whichever colors they wanted. I then rode and headed to the Takoma Park Post office not far the Metro Station, after I left the Silver Spring Post office with more packages left. I felt very comfortable taking another load at that post office also, because the short Asian lady who supervises that station is very friendly and helpful. I never had any problem with her no matter how many packages I had. Sometimes, I will take a certain amount to the counter when I had too many packages. But whenever she finishes what I brought to her, she will always ask me if I had some more left. Sometimes, she will be working at that post office alone with no help, but she loves her job and never treated me or any customer in a mean manner. But I had many bad experiences with some post office clerks at few other stations.

I GOT OUT OF HOMELESSNESS BY WORKING FOR MYSELF

It was a Saturday. The post office was quite empty. One or two customers showed up sporadically, but most of the time that I was inside, 30 minutes approximately, the two clerks behind the counter didn't have much work to do. I was happy. I had 18 packages of 3.70 pounds average each. They contained copies of my book that folks following me on social media, ordered. I have been to that post office for the last couple of years to ship book orders from my website. It was located on North Capitol and Massachusetts avenue. I never seen that lady before. She must have been new there, I guessed. I did not put the 18 packages in front of her at once but only put ten first. She processed them without any problem. I paid for them. She gave me my receipt. I looked behind me to check the line. They were nobody waiting. I grabbed the other packages that I had put on the counter and told her I had 8 more. She got upset and said, 'Why you ain't tell me you had more?" I only ended you 10 first because I did not want to hold the line in case somebody comes behind me. I don't see what the problem is. There is no customer waiting". I responded back and added. She became angrier and yelled at me "Next time, I'm not doing it". "Next time, I will have more than what I got now, and I will bring ten at a time until all my packages are processed" I retorted. She dropped the first package of the 8 that she was about to start and said" Guess what, I am not doing them" and walked away from the counter. I was shocked that she acted so mean for no reason. I guess she was enjoying a great time not doing too much work, until I came with 18 packages, and now, she had to get back to do some real work. I guess she was simply lazy. The other clerk watched without saying anything. But he told me that he was only taking cash payment. I stood there where the line started. Few customers came few minutes later. The other clerk processed their packages but would not do mine. I don't know whether they were all using cash only or not. I told him that I needed to talk their supervisor. He told me that she was gone for the day. I still stood there and everybody who came to the post office and lined up behind me were serviced by the clerk who was still at his counter. I pulled my phone and started video recording myself explaining what had happened, so that I could share it on my social media. The clerk walked away from his desk and went to the back and came right back after talking to somebody there. A lady walked from the back to the counter and asked me what the problem was. I explained what had happened. She went back and had the other clerk come back and process my orders. The clerk came back and started making up lies while doing my packages. She claimed that I disrespected her. She was a young lady, and I was obviously older than her. I felt that I was the one who was being disrespected. I explained to the supervisor that I had been homeless for a long time but was able to be successful a writing and selling my books online. I wanted her to understand why I have been coming to the post office with a lot of packages. And honestly, 18 packages were not that many. I had gone to many post offices with more packages than that, and the clerks had no problem processing them and asking me whether I had more when they finished. The supervisor told me to not let anybody stress me out like that. I told her I was diabetic and did not need that much stress. I stopped coming to that post office for a month or two after that incident. I preferred to go to the post offices in Silver Spring and Takoma Park instead. The clerks there were always nice and did not care how many packages I had. They processed everything I brought there anytime. Sometimes I had 40 packages. They did them all without getting upset or complaining.

One day, I don't know why I took my packages back to the post office on North Capitol Street after hesitating for a minute. She was at one of the counters when I entered. I decided to trust her this time to process my packages without giving me a hard time. It was during the holiday season. The post office was crowded this time. There were about 4 clerks behind the counter. Hers was the next available counter. I took my packages there. I only took ten of them, although I had more. I had a very important package to send by next day delivery express mail. I wanted it to get to destination before Christmas. The package contained three of my Always Remember That You Are A Wonderful Being hats. It was December 23. She told me that the package would be delivered on Christmas day. I went ahead and paid a little over $60 for the next day delivery shipping cost. The hats were ordered as Christmas presents by a couple for their kids. They wanted the hats to get there before Christmas. But when I checked with them, they texted me back to tell me that they did not receive the hats. The hats got to them two days after Christmas. It seems like the hats never left the post office before Christmas. I received a refund postal money order check for the amount I spent when I went back to complain. I am not accusing that clerk of having purposely mishandled my package and caused it to be delivered later than expected. But I just decided to never take my packages to her if I ever decided to go back there again.

But before that last incident with her, I had two other bad incidents with two other clerks at the same post office. Three clerks were working behind the counter, when I arrived there one day. One of them had also given me a hard time in the past. He always frowned when I came in with a lot of packages. I had about 15 of them. That was nothing compared to the 40 or sometimes 60 packages that I used to bring at one time. I took them instead to another lady who was new to me. I have never seen her there before. I greeted her and told her that my I was doing media rate shipping. "What is in them?" she asked. "Books" I answered. "What kind of books?" she kept asking me. "My books" I said to her. "Yes, but what kind of books are they? She kept on with her interrogations. I shook my head totally annoyed. "Look, I come here all the time and ship my books without problems. You can ask him, he knows me" I said and pointed at her co-worker, the one who also be mean to me. "I don't know you", he shouted. "Yes, you do" I responded. I was very disturbed by the unkindness of these folks towards me. I was not disrespectful to them, but they were just mean as if me bringing 10 or 20 or 30 packages was burdensome to them. I grabbed my packages and decided to take them to another post office. But while I was in another part of the lobby near the exit, I heard her explaining the situation to another clerk who witnessed what happened but pretended he was not paying any attention. She was not telling the truth, so I decided to walk back towards the counter and told her to tell the truth. "I told you that I had books in the packages, but you kept asking me the same questions over and over again about what was in the packages." Her response was that the packages felts like I had pamphlets in them. I shook my head because she was not making any sense. At that moment, another lady who never gave me any hard time and who was aware that some of her lady colleagues did, asked why I was leaving and told me to bring the packages. I praised her in front of the others and said that she was a good person, and she never gave me a hard time. She did all my 15 packages and asked if I had more. I did have more but I wanted to do 15 at that post office and then get on the train to another post office to do the rest. The lady did all of them as usual. I thanked and praised her for her professionalism and kindness.

I came back to that post office a month later because it was closer. I was next in line and the male clerk who said that he did not know me, was the one who was open next. I walked to him and greeted him. But he did not respond but acted very nasty, instead. "What is in them" He asked me. That man knew exactly that I had books in them. I had been bringing my book packages there so many times, for two years and he has processed them multiple times. "I got some books in them" I said calmly. He said he would only do 10 at time and I had to return to the back of the line to do the rest. I said no problem. I refused to give him back the same negative energy he was giving me. I refused to feed into his negative energy and allow it to affect me. I try to keep a positive energy inside me, no matter what negativity people sent towards me. He had an angry look on his face while he was processing my orders. I had less than 20 packages and I was going to get back in line anyway. I knew he wanted to be mean to me and was not going to do them all. The lady, who had given me a hard time the last time I was there, stopped by him and they had a conversation as if they were very close to each other. She was getting off work. She had three or four bags, that she laid on the floor by him. She asked him to bring them to her car, outside in front the post office. I immediately thought about helping her, but I was hesitant. I told him that I could take the bags outside to the lady. He was surprised and asked me if I wanted to do that. I said" off course." I grabbed the bags and took them out to the lady's car. She thanked me several times. The gentleman thanked me and told me that he really appreciated what I did. He asked me to bring all the packages that I had left. I did. He looked at me and apologized for having been mean to me all the time I did go there. I told him that it was ok, and he should not feel bad. I also said to him that, if I said anything in the past that ever offended him, I also apologize. He then asked me a little later whether I was the author of the books that I was shipping, I said yes.

The folks who supervise post offices in the Washington DC area, and that one in particular, take a minute every day to read the reviews on google from customers for each of their locations.

I want to share the reviews posted on the google search of that post office by a few customers who had the same experience as I, from probably the same clerks, to show that my experience there was not an exception:

Meghan Sebold, a week ago

The building is such a cool location and there is never a line, but the staff is so unnecessarily rude every time I go that I'm picking another location as my local USPS.

Channyn Williams 10 months ago

One had no idea what boxes they even had in stock when I asked another older clerk for help, her response was "They're over there. You didn't see them? They're literally right there" then proceeded to walk away as if I didn't just waste 10 minutes searching for a box they didn't even have after being told that they did. Complete waste of time. If you can use another location, you may want to do so.

ChristinaLoel 11 months ago

I wasn't going to write a review, but I've experienced too much bad energy here not to say anything. If you can drive to the next

USPS please do, some of the staff, no matter what time are always rude like we chose their profession. There's legit only one old gentleman with a pinky fingernail that is always nice no matter what, can't say the same for the others. The women always have attitudes, so I hope they either retire or get fired for complaints. That is all!

Briana Glover a year ago

Very unwelcoming and disrespectful and provided 0 customer service. A female clerk about 45+ stood talking to a customer for way longer than the transaction needed to complete. The customer had 1 package it was 650pm. I was in line with 2 other customers and the woman very much nasty stated she could not perform her duties of processing the correspondence because it was 7pm and she was ready to leave. These are the types of people who get hired to service guests such as myself. Please do better and put her on an earlier shift.

(Source: USPS 2 Massachusetts Ave NE, Washington DC)

I will admit that there are more positive than negative reviews for that post office. But my experience there has been stressful, unlike some other customers who have a better experience there.

I also had terrible experiences a couple of times at the Brentwood post offices with a few rude clerks. The last time, I went there, a young clerk gave me a hard time. I only had eight packages, but she told me that she was going to do only four and I had to get back in line. I told her that I come to the post office all the time, and I am always told that I can do ten packages at a time if there is a long line and return to back of the line with more packages. She told me I shouldn't tell her how to do her job. I responded that I was not trying to do that. He gave me a nasty look and said that I was being rude to her and that she would stop processing my packages. I told her that she is the one being mean for no reason and that I wanted to talk to her supervisor if she was not going to process my packages. She kept processing my orders then because she obviously was not trying to get the supervisor involved.

She then stopped after the third package and told me to step aside so that she could finish processing the package of the customer she had before me. The customer had stepped away to fill forms that was to be attached to her packages. The clerk should have finished processing mines and then get back to that customer, I thought. But I let her have it her way. After she finished that customer, she started chatting with one of her co-workers and took her time before resuming working on the rest of my packages. It was obvious to me that she was purposely trying to get on my nerves. I don't know what kind of pleasure she was experiencing being mean to me. I had a similar experience with two more clerks on different occasions, at that same post office.

I also want two of most recent reviews on google search for that post office, the Brentwood Post Office:

Erin Fairbanks a month ago

They don't even deserve one star. This facility is the absolute worst. The employees are Rude, surly, and are apparently too important to serve us, their postal customers. We are pests. How dare we ask about our mail and packages? Engaging with this facility is up there in unpleasantness with the DMV- actually, it may be worse.

I GOT OUT OF HOMELESSNESS BY WORKING FOR MYSELF

Graemme Boone 5 months ago

I wish I had read these reviews before I went. I had a TERRIBLE experience. The employee screamed at me, "I HATE THIS JOB!" I could tell she did. She threw my package towards the back of her counter. I was really surprised at her attitude during my transaction with her. I will not go back over there again. (Source Google reviews USPS 900 Brentwood Rd, NE Washington DC).

I may be mistaken, but I have noticed that folks who tend to provide poor customer service and display a mean attitude to customers look miserable and unhappy. This is why I try not to let their mean attitude towards me upsets and disturbs me. I just send positive energy towards them and wish that whatever issue is bothering them and making them unhappy get resolved. I stay happy no matter what I go through in life. I only have compassion and tolerance for those who are not nice to me as long as they don't go out of their way to cause me harm.

CHAPTER 6

BEING TOLERANT BECAUSE OF MY TERRIBLE EXPERIENCES

Being a self-published activist author is my full-time occupation. That means it is a job for me to write books to create awareness about homelessness and motivate and inspire others. I am therefore an entrepreneur since I am self-employed. I started selling my books on the street and later expanded to selling them online. I prefer to sell my books myself on my website, although amazon sends me 70 percent royalties every 60 days, for sales of my books on their website. Part of my work consists of growing my online audience. in order to generate more income and be able to keep a roof over my head and not be homeless again. I enjoy selling my books on the streets because I meet and interact with many people of all backgrounds and walks of life. But I also enjoy meeting and corresponding with new people who make up my audience on social media.

BEING TOLERANT BECAUSE OF MY TERRIBLE EXPERIENCES

As an activist and a motivational author, I try to reach everybody with my message. When I say everybody, I mean everybody, no matter what a person race, religion, ideology, social status and beliefs are. I understand that everybody had different opinions on the issue of homelessness, whether it is its causes or its solution, but I believe that each and all of us human beings should be aware and involved into efforts and actions to bring a solution to this issue. I also believe that we all deserve to be happy, no matter who we are, what we believe in, what we look like and whatever difference between us. I respect the differences among us, but I believe that we all have, in common, our humanity and desire to be happy and overcome difficulties.

I try my best to reach out to everybody and respect other people opinions whether I agree with them. I also try or not and try not to say or do anything that will offend them.

The most important thing to me is get everybody to become aware and to care about the issue of homelessness and get involved to help the homeless and end homelessness. I am aware that people will have different opinions according to what they believe or how they feel about homelessness and the homeless. But all I want to do is share my own experience with homelessness and hope that it gives them an additional understanding of that issue.

I try not to make assumptions about anybody reaction or feeling about homelessness and homelessness, because of their religion, ideology or other particular characteristics. And I try to have a neutral or a middle ground approach when I am in the midst of folks with differences. When I sell my books on the streets, I careless whether a person approaching me to check my books, is a Christian, Buddhist, Muslim, Atheist, or agnostic like me. It does not matter to me whether a person is an ideologically on the left, on the right or in the center. What matters to me is that we all have the same humanity in us.

I was selling my books on the streets one evening. Business was kind of slow. I was getting frustrated because nobody was stopping to buy my books, although there were a lot of people walking outside. I turned my head to my left towards the Washington Monument to see who was walking up from that side. I saw five or six young white males walking towards me. I say something to them. They came closer to hear what I was saying. I asked if they could support my books by buying a copy. They stopped and came and picked up few copies to see what the book was about. When they got close enough, I noticed that each of them had a confederate flag on either their belts' buckle or buttons pinned to their jackets. It was clear to me that they were most likely part of a group of protesters, who were in town to oppose the removal of the confederate flag in public places. They did not seem to be bothered by my skin color, although they could easily be stereotyped as white supremacists, because they were wearing the confederate flag on them. A couple of them purchased a copy of my book. I have sold a lot of books during rallies and protests, from both pro-republicans and pro-democrat rallygoers. One day, I was out there selling my books. It was a Friday, I think. There were crowds of folks everywhere walking up and down the street. Most of the folks came to DC to participate in two separate rallies that were to take place each of one of the next two days. I knew that one of the rallies was a pro-life March for folks opposing abortion. Pro-life marchers are Republicans in majority. Many of them were wearing Trump's red Let's Make America Great Again campaign slogan baseball caps. The other march was a Million Woman March, which was organized by groups affiliated with the Democratic party. The march was an anti-Trump event.

I was out there trying to sell my books to each and all of the folks out there. To me homelessness was an issue that should concern everybody, whether they were in town to support or oppose Trump or for or against abortion or Republicans or democrats. An older couple stopped in front of my books to get a copy. We are in town for the rally tomorrow. I told them that there were two rallies going on that week end. The man said "No, no! We are not here for the crazy people's rally!" I didn't know which rally they were in town for. So, I did not know what to say, because I did not want to say anything that would offend them. "We are here for the pro-life rally" he said. I signed their copies and wished their rally a success. Few hours later, two middle aged ladies stopped to buy my book. I only had my first book Homeless Lives Matter then. "We here for the rally" they also said, when I asked them if they were visiting from out of town. "We are here for the good rally. The other folks are crazy" she said. I wasn't sure who she was talking about, but she made it clear by expressing her disdain for Trump and thought his supporters were out of their mind. I wish a success to their rally as well, after I signed their copy. In situations like that, I have to be careful not to offend any person by voicing my opinion on what their belief or when I don't know where they stand. I only listen to them respectfully and keep mine to myself. Now if I agree with them, off course, I will say something in support. But if I disagree, I will not antagonize them, because I want them to also show empathy for the homeless and speak against homelessness, no matter where they stand, when it comes to politics, ideology or religion.

I sell my books on 15th and G street, right across the treasury department and not far from the White House. On many occasions, I caught President Donald Trump and Joe Biden's motorcades riding by me, on their way in or out of the White House.

Whenever I am out there selling my books, I always stand up, grab my phone and videotape any protest march that goes up or down on 15th street, from or to the White House, sometimes from or to the US Capitol. But I stay close enough to my books. That particular day in June, there was a rally to protest the supreme court decision to reverse Roe Vs Wade. I saw the protest walking up on 15th street towards the White House. It looked like they were coming from the Supreme Court building. I got up as I normally do and stood on the sidewalk to watch the March. One of the protesters who had a mike and was in front of a group in the March came close to the sidewalk and screamed at the bystanders. it looked like she was looking at me directly. She admonished us for standing on the sidewalk instead of joining the march. I posted the video on my Instagram page homelesslivesmatterbook. Some of the readers agreed with the protester. They commented that since I am an activist myself, I should have joined the march, in solidarity with other activists since they were obviously allies.

Fact of the matter is that I could not join the march, even if I wanted to. I was out there selling my books on the sidewalk. I had too much stuff to carry and could not just pack up and join the march. I should have just made that comment and leave the issue alone. But I was foolish enough to want to explain my position on the issue of abortion. I basically said that I was pro-choice but not necessarily for abortion, and that I agreed that it is a woman right to decide to keep or terminate her pregnancy and should not be jailed for doing so. But at the same time, I would encourage a woman to keep the pregnancy or give the baby up for adoption instead of aborting it. There are a lot of women out here who cannot give birth but would love to adopt a child and take good care of it. If a pregnant woman can change her mind on and let another woman keep the baby, that can be a great thing. If she doesn't want to abort, then that is her choice and should not be punished for that. My position was a way to bridge both adverse positions on the issue. I know how passionate both the pro-life and pro-choice activists and protesters are on how they feel about abortion. I understand both sides and I see the validity in both position to a certain degree. My position is a way to show to both sides that I see their points, but I do not necessarily agree that one side is totally right and the other totally wrong. I believe not everything is hundred percent right or wrong and not everything is black of white. There is grey also in between. My thing is that there are pro-life and pro-choice folks who are out there helping the homeless and engaged in the fight against homelessness. I do not want to offend anybody on either side. The fight against homelessness is universal and transcends ideological, religious, racial, ethnic and political affiliations. Unfortunately, many of my followers stopped following me. I lost about 300 followers after that post. That kind of really hurt me. I never explained why I have this position when it comes to abortion. It is a very personal issue to me although I am not a woman. I am a biological father of a daughter who is 27 years old. I never mentioned her in my writings and posts on social media. I also have an adopted daughter with whom I have a close father daughter relationship. I want to explain why I have the position that I have when it comes to abortion. Once again, I believe that it is a woman's right to choose to keep her pregnancy or not, but if she asks my opinion, I will advise her to keep it or give it to adoption. But if she doesn't want to, that is her choice, and no government should jail her for that. I know some pro-life and some pro-choice will not accept my position because I am on both sides while disagreeing with both sides. Here is the reason why.

I was at the Martin Luther King Library in the spring of 2002 or a year before that. I am not sure. I had left the shelter at the trailers that was located on Kendall street in Ivy City, a neighborhood in North East Washington DC. I went to kill time at the Library since I was homeless. It was an overnight shelter. We had to leave with all our belongings at 7 am and check back in at 5pm. I walked on New York avenue for twenty good minutes to SOME to get breakfast and take a shower, then I went to the library and waited till they opened. This was my routine when I decided to just chill and not go on a day job to make some money working as laborer on construction sites. I had signed to use the computer and was waiting for the next one available. She did also. I got on a computer. She did also. She was trying to print out a document. She asked for my help. I did help her print whatever she needed to. We ended up becoming friends. I liked her. I thought she liked me to. We met at the library the next day. She invited me to her place. I went there. She had two kids, a daughter who was about 8 years old and a son who was about 5years old. We were intellectually attracted to each other's mind. We enjoyed each other's company. We spent time into long conversations that ended up into passionate debates. She had lost her job and was sending applications to several places. I had no job but was going to day jobs from time to time to work on construction sites. I never told her that I was staying in the shelter. She had a two-bedroom apartment. Both of her kids were sharing a bedroom and she was staying in the second one. But she had a futon sofa bed in her living room in addition to a dining table, a sofa, and a loveseat, I think. The first night I spent at her house, we talked all night. It was a week end. She had sent her kids to spend few weeks of summer with her mother in New York. So, when I went to her place the second night, it was only me and her in the apartment. She questioned me about why I never told her where I live. She wondered if I had a girlfriend and was hiding it from her. I told her that I was homeless and was staying at the shelter. I asked if that was going to be a problem as far as the relationship that we started was concerned. She had no problem with it. She asked me to move in with her. I was not too sure if I wanted to do that. But I stayed overnight. We got intimate while conversing in the dark. The attraction was intense. When I laid on top of her as we were locked in each other's arms, she pushed me away and started crying. I moved back, held her and asked her what was wrong. She kept crying frantically. I kind of guessed what was happening but I wanted her to feel comfortable enough to tell me. I sat up on the sofa bed, held her and tried to comfort her. "What is wrong?" I asked her while caressing her back. "Ok, you don't have to explain until you feel comfortable enough to tell me". I said. She calmed down after a while and explained to me that she was raped by the father of her son and got pregnant from the rape. She and him were best friends. I am not sure if they also were co-workers. But he had a wife and was having some marital issues. She explained how that happened. They were very close friends. He gave her a ride one day and when they got into her place, he forced himself on her and raped her. That is what she told me. She said that after that incident, she never could engage into sex with the person that she dated later. She was single when the incident happened. She said the guy who she was in a relationship with before she met me was very understanding and very respectful and accepted that she had problem having sex with him, because of what she had gone through with the father of her child. The relationship with her boyfriend ended. She was single when we met. I left in the morning after that incident. I came to see her a couple of days later. When I wanted to leave to return to the shelter in the evening, she wanted me to spend the night with her. I accepted. We got intimate again and got on top of each other. When I was about to initiate sex, she started crying again. She wanted to do it but just couldn't. I told her" Listen, I am not the one who raped you. You have to overcome that problem, otherwise the man who did that to you still have total control over you mentally. If you care for me, you have to break that control and do what you want to do. You can't keep giving him the power to prevent you from being intimate with a person that you care for" I told her. She cried and held me, and we had sex. After that, we became inseparable. She didn't want me to go back to the shelter. I stayed with her. Her kids came back from New York. They had met me before they left to spend part of the summer with their grandmother in New York. They seemed ok with me being living in the house with them. He son adopted me as his father. He looked at me one day and said, "you, my daddy." I was very disturbed and pained by the story of how he came in this word. I took him to kindergarten every morning and went to pick him up. His mother got a job as a teacher. I was going through a lot at the time. She ended up getting pregnant by me. She asked me to marry her. I wasn't sure if I was ready for that. I loved her so much and was so happy to be with her. But I did not have myself together. I was living in her place and did not have a place of my own. I was dealing with my own traumas that I will not share here for now. Maybe in my next book. It was summer and we decided to go to New York for a week to visit her mother. Two days after we got there, her mother asked me to take a ride with her to the store. While on the way there, she asked me when I was going to marry her daughter? She knew her daughter was 4 months pregnant from me. I was very nervous and disturbed. I told her mother that I loved her daughter, but I did not have myself together yet, and I was going through a lot, and it would be premature to get married at the time, but I did want to marry her daughter. We returned to the house. My girlfriend and I spent a lot of time on the beach on Long Island, sometimes, the entire night. We returned to Washington DC a week later. A week after that, she and I had an argument early in the morning while we were in the living room on the couch. She got up and told me that her mother told her that I did not want to marry her. She got up early in the morning the next day and told me to look after her kids, and that she had to go to an appointment and would be right back. I waited all day long, fixed breakfast, dinner and lunch for her daughter and son and had them go to bed at night. She came in very late, around 11 pm. She was very sad when she came in. I asked her if she was ok. She started crying and held me. I asked her what was wrong. She told me that she just had an abortion. She was five months pregnant. I was totally devastated but I did not react in anger. She went to her son's room and went to sleep on his bed with him. He was already asleep, so was her daughter. I slept in the living room by myself. In the morning, I went inside the bathroom and shaved my hair. I had long dreadlocks, like hers. I felt disgusted with myself. I really wanted the son, but I understood why she did what she did. She was already raising two kids by herself. The son who never knew his father and the daughter who had no relationship with her father. So, I was the father of the two kids. I wanted to leave and go back to the homeless shelter, but I also wanted to be there for her for few more days until she healed from the procedures. That was a late-term abortion. Whether I agreed with the mother's right to choose or not, a four to five months pregnancy is not the same as a one-to-two-month pregnancy, especially when you are the father of that child. I felt like I had just lost a son. My biological son. I left and went to the shelter after a couple of days. I did not have a phone then. She had a house phone. There was a payphone by the trailers at the shelter. She had the number. And also, she knew where to meet me. When I was not going to do some construction work, I was at the Martin Luther King Library. She came to meet me there one day, a week after I left. She told me that her son missed me a lot. She said that every night he refused to go to bed and stood by the door to wait for me to come in, until he falls asleep by the door, and she picks him to take him to his bed. I was kind of saddened by that. The boy was very attached to me. He was like a real son to me although not biologically. He never had a man to relate to in the house until I moved in. He only had his mother and his sister. He even sounded a bit effeminate because he was imitating his mother and sister, even their feminine way of speaking. He used to wear their women shoes and he even kind of look like a little girl. When I used to walk him to school on my shoulders, some folks would say" she is a cute little girl". I would respond," he is a boy" and they would apologize. I was a bit concern by that. But I noticed a progressive change in his behavior. He seemed like he was becoming more and more masculine in his ways the more I was around. His voice become lower pitch and stronger. He tended to imitate me more and more. I thought he was making a difference between being a man and being a woman because I was living with him, his mother and his sister as the only man in the house and his father figure. I reinforce that by having him flex his muscle and playing with him by making him say, making him say "I'm a man" with authority and with a loud voice with a bass voice. He stopped wearing his sister and mother's shoes and stopped acting like a girl.

I could therefore relate to his mother's concerns, and I understood that I should not interrupt the interaction with her son because the boy had got attached to me as a son to his father. I did not develop the same closeness with her daughter. She even became a little affected by the fact that I was not playing a lot with her and giving her the same attention as I was giving her brother. I played a lot with the boy because I wanted him to be a bit more aggressive and not be soft. I lifted him up in the air and tossed him in the couch and he loved it. Or I will grab both of his hands and spin him around in the air. He will come back for me to keep doing it although it was scary. The girl started being sad and will tell her mother that I did not like her and cry about it. But the reality is that I was a bit more cautious not to have too much physical contact with the girl. I did not want anything physical playfulness to be misconstrued as some kind of sexual contact. But the child did not understand why I would not lift her up and put her on my shoulder and spin around like I did with her brother. Also, the boy was more obedient to me. When he does something wrong and I tell him to stop, he obeyed. The daughter was a bit disobedient, and I just left her alone when I tell her to stop doing something that her mother would not allow her to do. For example, I use to bake a cake and gave them the portion their mother wanted me to give them until she gets home. The daughter will go to get more slices without my permission and will pay me no mind when I reminded her that her mother told me not to let them have more than she was having. One day, I told her to stop doing something that she was not supposed to do. But she was recalcitrant and told me" You are not my father; you don't tell me what to do". I got offended by that, and that made me more reluctant to play with her.

Let's get back to the mother. She said that even if we were not together anymore, she wanted me to still come and see her son. I promised that I would. I started going there, but when it was time for me to go back to the shelter, she insisted that I spent the night there. I decided not to keep going there because we were back getting intimate again and a bit too much. I was afraid that I was going to get her pregnant again and the baby could have ended up getting aborted again. I was back at the shelter in CCNV at second and D street, North West Washington DC. I had a permanent bed there, and I was going on a day job every day. I wanted to stay at the shelter and focus on working on myself. The abortion of the child that I really wanted disturbed me a lot.

About a week after I stopped going to her place, I received a message at the shelter. The message said that I had to call her urgently. I went to her place. She was not feeling well. She was laying in her couch, holding her stomach while moaning and sobering. tears and moaning. She was having terrible abdominal pains. I called 911. An ambulance came and got her. I kept the kids in the house and called her mother. She had residue from the abortion in her uterus. She stayed in the hospital for two days. They cleaned her womb of the remains of the aborted baby that was still in her womb. I stayed with her for a month or two after that but left, after she told me one day, that she loved me but could not respect a man who could not take care of his woman. I felt embarrassed and ashamed, but I agreed with her. I was not responsible enough. I did not deserve her.

I did not tell her that I was going to leave for good. I got up in the morning and told her that I had to go handle some business, and I would be back. I went to get a permanent bed at the CCNV shelter. I came back in the evening. She asked me where I had been. I did not answer. She put her kids to bed and came back in the living room. She wanted us to go lay down. I told her that I was not going to stay anymore because I agreed with her. I told her that I did not think I deserved her and that I was going to stay in the shelter and work on myself. She told me that I run away from my responsibilities. He son was like my son, so me leaving was like abandoning him. I felt bad about it, but I had to move on with my life because I had to try to solve the issues that I was dealing with.

Few months later, I moved out of the shelter to a rooming house. I was renting a room there for $75 a week. It was located on the corner between Rhode Island and 4th street, North West. I was going to work on construction sites every day.

I ended up leaving the place after a year because when I came from work one day, there was no electricity in the building. One of the guys who stayed there also told me that there was an electric fire in the building and the firemen had to go to the top of the building through the roof in my room. I opened my door and when I looked towards the roof, I could see the sky. The landlord did not bother to have the hole covered. I had to go outside and found some plywood and carboard and use them to cover the over the hole. I left after that.

He was still collecting rent every Friday although we stayed in the darkness with no electricity for two weeks while I still had the hole in the roof above me not fixed.

I was at the Martin Luther King Library one day. I ended up in the company of a lady who was also homeless. We sat at the same table and started conversing. We became friends. I was back at the shelter in the trailers in Ivy City. She was also staying at a woman shelter. I don't know why she was homeless. She could go and stay at her mother's home uptown off Georgia Avenue, anytime she wanted to. But she preferred to stay in shelters. Her sister and her brother were staying at the house with her mother. She had two sons that were adopted. I never knew the reasons why. But she had a good relationship with them. I was stressed out and depressed, because I really did not like staying at the shelter. Sometimes I was put in a trailer that was smelling very bad. The trailers had I think eight bunk beds in them. There was a space at the bottom in the middle and on top. Some of the guys did not take care of their hygiene. When they took, they shoes off, the smell took over the entire trailer. I had migraines sometimes because I could not stand smelling other people stinking feet all night. There was a payphone by the trailers. She called me at the payphone every night before going to sleep. We met at the library later in the day. One night, she told me that she talked to her mother about me, and that I was welcome to go spend the night in her mother's living room, every time I felt depressed in the shelter and could not sleep. I had not met her mother yet so, I told her that I would go there only with her. We started going to sleep at her mother house now and then. We stayed in the living room. Her mother lived upstairs. Her brother was in the basement, and her sister had the other bedroom. We were not going there every day but a day or two in the week.

She was a devoted Christian. I was an agnostic. She was trying to get me to go to church. I respectfully declined. One night, she called me when I was in the shelter. She wanted me to come and stay with her at her mother's. I really was stressed about a lot of things and was not really trying to get into a commitment when I heard her talking about marriage. I was homeless, she was homeless. Marriage was the last thing on my mind. I could not take care of myself. How would I be able to take care of a woman? I was still traumatized by the previous experience I had with the 5 five-month pregnant former girlfriend who had the abortion. I told myself after that experience that I don't deserve to be in a relationship with a woman if I don't have the means to take care of both of us.

The lady on the phone was disturbed and did not understand why I acted like I did not want to be with her. I told her that I was depressed about my life and was not really ready to commit to a relationship as a homeless person. She told me that she was pregnant. I got depressed when I heard that. I told her that I was not ready to have a kid, and that she should have an abortion since she was only a month of two pregnant. She said that as a Christian, she did not want to do that. I was totally distressed and confused and depressed. I didn't know what to do. I stopped taking her calls, whenever someone will come to the trailer to tell me that I had a call from her. I moved out of the shelter and stopped going to the library or anywhere where I would run into her. I saw her one day, a year later. She was at the bus stop On 7th and Rhode Island St. She had a job and moved back to her mother's house. Her mother had passed away. I was sad to hear that, but I was happy to see her. She was not mad at me, but she was not answering my questions totally. She told me that I hurt her feelings by leaving her like that. I apologized to her. I told her that I still love her, but I was going through a lot then and was too stressed out. I asked her what happened to the pregnancy that she had. She answered, "don't worry about it". I insisted. She told me that I asked her to have an abortion, and I didn't want her when she told me that she was pregnant. So, I should not worry about what happened after that. Because I knew she was a devoted Christian, I kind of doubted that she really had the abortion. I kept asking her if she did keep the pregnancy and had a child. She said, 'don't worry about her, she is ok". Then she repeated again that she did have an abortion. I was very confused because she mentioned "Her" as if she meant that she had a girl from the pregnancy. I asked for her number, she refused to give it to me. Her bus came, she got on it and left. Up to today, I don't know if she really had an abortion or a child by me.

BEING TOLERANT BECAUSE OF MY TERRIBLE EXPERIENCES

CHAPTER 7

HOMELESSNESS IS NOT A CHOICE

I feel like I am accomplishing something in my life, when my work inspires and motivates readers of my books and give them the desire to get involved with the issue of homelessness.

Messages like this one that I received on March 13, 2023, from Billy in Australia, humble me and make me commit more to my work.

He purchased my book Homeless Lives Matter, Homeless My story from me on the street, a month earlier.

"Hi Leo, I don't know if you remember me but I'm the Australian who bought a copy of your book from you in early January. I wanted to let you know that I just finished reading it and it was really quiet eye opening. Even on the other side of the world it's clear there's room for many of your experiences, thoughts, and ideas to be applied here too. Thanks for painting this issue in a new light for me, I will strive to be more compassionate and a bigger advocate for homeless rights than I was before. Billy".

I feel like society has become more apathetic towards the homeless and poor people in general. There are more and more homeless individuals and their tents visible on the streets, and society seems to have accepted it as normal. There is no public outrage about it. I think we should try to help and support and be more compassionate and not always try to condemn others for their predicament.

I rushed to the metro station at Rhode Island Avenue to get on the next train to Silver Spring on my way home. It was 7:26pm. I was about to tap my card on the gate to get in. At the same time, my attention was drawn by a gentleman who was very upset. He looked like he was in his late 20's or early 30's. He had Puerto Rican or Dominican features. He kept looking around on the floor and walked half-way towards the station entrance and turned back around. He asked the attendant whether he had seen a phone that he said he lost. He described it. The attendant answer was negative. He entered the station behind me. He approached me as I was about to get on the escalator and asked me if he could use my phone to call his sister. He told me that she had just bought him the phone the same day. He did not memorize the phone number, so he wanted her to call her to see if she could locate it.

I know what it feels like to lose a phone. I myself had lost my phone on the train a month earlier. I exited the train but realized that I did not have my phone on me, when I went downstairs to exit the station. The train had left by then and was heading towards the next station on the way to Glenmont Station, its final destination about 4 stations away. The attendant asked me to get back on the platform upstairs and wait for the train to return back in the next five minutes. I tried to remember which car I should get in and check, when the train came back in the opposite direction. But I thought it was a waste of time, since I could not remember exactly which car, I was in. The train had 6 cars. But I was fortunate enough because a lady passenger found it. I went to purchase another phone the next day and was able to get in touch with her and get my phone back. I gave her $40.

I normally feel apprehensive about letting a stranger use my phone in a public place, but I felt sorry for him.

I handed him my phone and stood close enough. He called his sister, but the call went straight into the answering service. He tried to call again a couple of time, but he was out of luck. He left a message on the answering service. He then handed me my phone back and thanked me. But I heard him say something about going to the shelter, when he was leaving a message on her answering service. I asked him where he was staying. He answered that he was staying at a shelter in Rockville. He thanked me again and headed to the escalator. I called him back and handed him the money I had on me. It was not much. Maybe $8 or $9. "That's for me?" He said. " Yes. I used to be homeless for over ten years. So, we together man " I added. When I got to the top on the platform, he told me" look, I need to tell you this. You gave me this money, but I feel bad because I am an addict and I will most likely get high with it, although I already some stuff on me". He did not tell me what he was addicted to and what he had on him, but I assumed that he was talking about crack cocaine. I know a lot of people are conflicted whether to give or not to a homeless begging them for money, because they assume that the homeless person may use the money for alcohol or drug instead of food. I think that unless you know for certain that the money you give will be misused, you should not make assumptions about what a person is going to do with it. Now, if a person comes to you and tells you that he needs some money to get a drink or get high, or if you know for sure that he or she will use your money to get drunk or high, then you will make your decision to give to them or not, based on the facts and not on assumption.

I answered" look, you are fine, don't feel bad, I am not here to judge you. I just hope that one day, you get some help with your addiction. But don't feel bad. I gave it to you, and it is yours." I wanted him to keep the money, because he was honest enough to tell me that he had an addiction problem after I gave him the $8 or $9. Sometimes we don't know why people get addicted to alcohol or drugs. This is why I prefer to show compassion and help the best I can, instead of condemning a person who is sick. All I can do is comfort and encourage him to seek help.

Homelessness is not a choice and ending it is not easy

I was watching a video on the YouTube channel of a vlogger from outside the US, who was visiting Washington DC. She was shocked to see so many homeless people on the streets. She made a video about it near the homeless camp that was in McPherson Square, the park on 15th St in downtown Washington. In the video, she said that she was told by her friends who reside in the Washington DC area that most of the homeless choose to be homeless and refuse to be housed or to work. I wish I had met her and given her my book Homeless Lives Matter, Homeless My Story, so that she could know that most of what she was told are stereotypes that I dispelled in the book. I already addressed the issue in my first book. So, I won't repeat everything in this book again. But let's me say this. I disagree with folks who claim that most people who are homeless choose to be homeless.

To think that all homeless people are either drug addicts, mentally ill or unwilling to work and therefore are making a conscious choice to be homeless, is not the right way to understand homelessness.

The problem with people who don't want to feel sorry for the homeless and only want to blame them for what they are going through, is that they only think of homeless people as drug addicts, mentally ill and lazy people who prefer to leave outside than go to work.

It is a fact that a great number of homeless visible on the streets of major US cities including Washington DC, are the mentally ill, drug or alcohol addicts and unemployed ones. But, truth of the matter, is that there are more homeless men and women and young folks who are not mentally ill, drug addicts or unemployed. They are not the ones who people see every day on the street corner. They are the invisible homeless. They dress nicely and look clean and blend in with normal people. You ride the bus or the subway with them every day, or sit at coffee shops next to them while they are working on their laptop and you have no idea that they are homeless. They go to work every day, but their co-workers don't even know that they are homeless. Unfortunately, the stereotypical idea of a homeless person is the mentally ill, the drug addict, the unemployed who hangs in parks or sleep outside. But many homeless sleep in their cars, on a friend's couch or even in the tents downtown when they sneak in them at night without anybody noticing them.

To say that they are homeless because they are lazy and don't want to work is incorrect and unfair. Many homeless folks do have a job or go to work every day, but they are not earning enough to afford rent, in a city where cost of living is high and living wage is higher than minimum wage. That means that a lot of homeless who earn minimum wage cannot afford cost of living here in Washington DC. So having a job is not necessarily a remedy for homelessness if the job is not paying enough to afford cost of living in this expensive city.

The majority of unemployed, alcoholics, drug and substance addicts, mentally ill are not homeless. Also, many of them are your friends, neighbors, co-workers, or relatives.

I don't think that homeless people who have issues with drug or alcohol addiction, mental illness, unemployment, and some other issue, deserve to be homeless. Until you know why they are on the street and what they went through in life, do not judge the homeless, that you see out there struggling with addiction, mental illness, unemployment, and other issues prevalent in the homeless communities.

Pastor who disrespected my dead homeless friend

I could not make it to her funeral, because I had a doctor's appointment at about the same time. But, I was shocked when I heard the Pastor officiating over the funeral make these statements: "Drinking and drugging and sexing and lying and cheating and stealing and gossiping and just being a simple plain whore or a pimp or a pusher... Rhonda and others in this room, look at the F's that has been in her life an your life, fun, food, shopping, which represent finances, family, faith, we forget .... any woman, there is no way of getting out of it, god gives your life, he gives you the opportunity to spend this life on his side, or on the other side. "This was what the pastor said about my friend in what is supposed to be an eulogy. Why would he think that it was ok to talk about a deceased person laying in a coffin in front of him and in the presence of her two teenage kids, her mother, her sister and brother and the rest of her family and friends attending the service? The service was broadcasted on the church YouTube channel. I watched it as soon as I left the clinic. I saved it on my laptop which I had with me.

My friend was a homeless woman who had just got housed for few months. Her dead body was found decomposed in her studio apartment by the building maintenance worker, a week after she returned there after being missing for a month.

One day in mid-October 2021, I received a call from her younger sibling. She told me that she and her family were looking for Rhonda, who was missing since she left her apartment on Sept 30 and has not been seen or heard from since.

The last time I heard from Rhonda was few days before she went missing. She had called me 6 or 8 times that night. The calls woke me up. I looked at the number but did not feel like answering. I meant to call her later. But I was neglectful and only called her a few days later, but her phone was off. I even texted her one of my Instagram inspirational messages. But I never heard back from her, until her sister called me and asked me if I had seen or talked to her recently. I had never met or talked to her sister before. But I did have several phone conversations with her mother, many times a couple of years before. Rhonda was going through some challenges, and I was trying to help her the best I could, whenever she reached out to me.

She was one of two female homeless friends that knew where my tent was, and who I allowed to come there and stay for a few nights, when they wanted to get away from situations and people that they had issue with. I trusted her. I knew she would not tell anybody where my tent was. She has just left an abusive relationship with a homeless man. I met her around SOME House, where the homeless used to go for breakfast, lunch, and other services. She ended up in another relationship with another homeless person. She called me several times to tell me that she was coming to my tent when he needed to get away from her boyfriend when he was giving her a hard time. He had her living with him in a shack in the backyard of his mother's house. She told me that she was not allowed inside the house. Her boyfriend used to leave her in the shack by herself for a day or two, with no food or money. When she got tired of waiting for him, she walked outside the place and got on the bus with no money to the train station nearby. She asked someone who had a phone to let her make a phone call. She called me and told me that she was coming to my tent to get away because she had enough. She showed up in my tent around 2 am, many times. She stayed in my tent for a couple of days and told me that she had to go visit her kids at her mother's place not very far from where my tent was located. One day, I was staying at a friend's girlfriend's apartment not far from my tent. My friend girl's friend was staying with him and had left her apartment vacant. I paid her $40 every three days to stay there. I stayed there for 3 to 4 weeks. Rhonda called me one day and told me that she needed to come and stay in the tent. I told her that I was staying in a friend's apartment. She came there the same afternoon. She told me that the man was too abusive to her, and she really had enough that time and she was not going back. She told me that he wanted to stay with me. I told her that I was in that apartment temporarily and that I was not supposed to have anybody with me there. I had another homeless lady friend there to. I mentioned her in a story in a previous chapter. Rhonda cried. She told me that she had nowhere to go and did not want to go back to the same guy. I told her that I loved her dearly, but I could not take care of her and that she needed to go to a domestic violent organization that would help her get a place. She told me that she would go to the court building in the morning to file a stay away order and get some help from there. I gave her some transportation money to go the court the next morning.

I doubted that she would do it. I did not hear from her for a couple of days. Then she called me the third from a detox program located inside the former DC general hospital. She told me that she was going to a drug rehab program and from there she will be enrolled into a temporary and then permanent housing program. She told me to call her mother and tell her that she was going to a drug rehab to get herself together. She ask me to be there for her while she is in the program. I promised that I would. I never interacted or met her mother before. But I called her. She was not very optimistic. She told me that her daughter had been in many drug treatment programs before, but it never worked. I told her to be optimistic and that I know her daughter is trying very hard, and it is not easy on her. A week or so later, she got placed into a drug program in Washington DC although she told me that she was going to a drug program in Florida. I brought her some packs of cigarettes and clothes regularly. She called me one day to tell me that her boyfriend came there one day to argue with her although she had a stay away order on him. She said that she was going to be moved to another program. A few days later, I sent a friend to bring her some cigarettes and whatever she needed, but he was told that she had walked away from the program. I was very disappointed. Her mother was right, I told myself.

A month or two later, she showed up in my tent. She was remorseful. I don't know why I left the program. she told me. The purpose of her going to the program was to work her way into permanent housing. But now, she was back to square one. I asked her what happened. She told me that she had met a guy while at the detox and they were sent to the same drug treatment program. She felt in love with him. He told her that he had his own apartment and that they should leave the program and go to stay together. He and her got back getting high. They ended up int a very dangerous situation because the man was beaten and threatened to get hurt if he did not pay a drug bill he had with some folks in the neighborhood. I encouraged her to return to another program. She promised me that she would, and she did.

She completed the program and was put into a temporary shelter for women victims of domestic violence somewhere in downtown DC, if my memory serves me right. I don't know what happened later because we lost touch.

She got in touch with me months later. I was staying at my friend in Trinidad, a neighborhood in the easter art of

Washington DC. She asked me for some money because she needed some cigarettes. I asked her where she was. She told me that she was staying with a new boyfriend in the Trinidad neighborhood as well. I rode my bike down the street and met her on the street where she was staying and handed her $20. I told her that I would pay her to help me do some work. She told me no problem. She rushed back to the house and told me that she would come and help me anytime I was ready and also talk to me because she was going through some stressful situation. I told her that I needed some help anyway because I had a lot of books to process and ship. That was when I had over 1000 orders that came in during the fundraiser, I made on my social media around my 55th birthday in November 2020.

She knew where my friend's building was. she had met me there before in the past. She told me that her previous boyfriend was still harassing her, although he had a court ordered stay-away order on him. . He was hanging around the place where she and her newest boyfriend lived. She also told me that she was disappointed at her new boyfriend as well. He was becoming deceitful and abusive. A lady that he claimed was his former girlfriend was coming to their place and bang on the door while she was home alone and her boyfriend at work. She felt harassed. She believed that boyfriend was still involved with the woman. She confronted him one day. He admitted that he was still messing with her because she was giving him money and helping him when he was in need, but he did not care about her. Sher did not buy that.

So, Rhonda was growing displeased with her new relationship, but she felt compelled to force herself to stay with him while working on getting her own place. She came and helped me processing my orders. I paid her about $20 per hour. She worked for 6 hours the first day. I gave her $120. She came early around 6 am the next day and did the same. On the third day, she told me that she had to go meet with her father to take care of some business. The following day, she showed up and told me that she would not stay long because she had to go with her case manager about her housing. Less than two hours after she started working on my laptop, her phone kept rigging. Her boyfriend kept calling her and asking her when she would finish. She kept telling him that she would finish and come home soon. He kept calling her every ten minutes. I was wondering what was going on. About an hour later, she told me that she had to leave and will come back to finish a couple of hours later. I gave her $60 for the three hours she worked on my laptop processing my orders. She never came back. I have not heard from her for two days and she did not pick up my phone when I called. I did the work by myself. I had to process orders, package the books ordered, stick address labels on all the packages and then take them to the post office. I had over a thousand orders to process. It was a lot of work. She was pretty fast at processing the orders. I was slower. I started missing her. She called me on the third day. I told her before she came that if she could not stay for at least four hours, then I did not need her. She promised that she would. She told me that she wanted to be honest with me and tell me about a serious problem that she had but asked me not to be mad at her. I told her that I would not. She explained to me that when the boyfriend kept calling her, it was because he wanted her to bring the money that she was making, so he could buy some heroin. He had a heroin addiction. She revealed to me that he had her try. She thought she had got addicted to it as well, although she had never done heroin in her life before. I knew she had a crack cocaine addiction and was also smoking K2 spice also known as synthetic cannabinoids. It is a cheap drug that is prevalent in homeless communities. It is made of a mixture of spices and herbs sprayed with chemicals. A lot of homeless smoke it. It used to sell for $2 a joint and goes for $5 now. She told me in the past that she started smoking marijuana when she was younger, then got into smoking PCP. PCP is made of animal tranquilizer, embalming fluid or even rocket fuel. She told me that she got taken to a mental institution after smoking some PCP one time. But I know she was not messing with PCP or marijuana the time I knew her. I told her that she needed to go get some help because heroin was too dangerous a drug for her to get addicted to. She was sniffing it and not shooting it. But still, heroin addiction is hard to get rid of.

She did go back into a drug program and got into her new apartment soon after. She already had a housing voucher but was waiting for the inspection and the process to complete. She called me one day to ask me for some money. I got upset at her because she had not told me that she had finally moved to her new place, until 3 to 4 weeks later and also because she wanted me to meet her at the Walmart near her building. "Why can't I meet you at your new apartment?" I asked her. She claimed that she had relatives visiting her and resting at her place. I knew she was being truthful. It was obvious to me that she had one the same guy who had got her addicted to heroin move in with her. I asked her about it, she denied it. She called me a few weeks later and invited me to her new place. I noticed some men shoes in the entrance of her studio. She told me the truth that she had her last boyfriend there, but she had to put him out after they got into arguments, and he put his hands on her. I admonished her and told her that she had to stop messing with the same guys who are abusing her and not helping her become better. But she had her previous boyfriend who she had a stay away order against, move in with her. That was the start of her doom. The guy ended up in an accident and got hospitalized. He had her building's front entrance door and elevator's keys. She could not get inside her building unless someone let her in. She visited him at the hospital, but he did not give her the keys. She spent more time outside in the tents of some of her homeless friends, under the bridge or in the park and getting high. She had called me one day to ask me if I was ready to have her come and help me process some of my book orders. I had told her that I had got a lot of orders and needed her help to process them as she did in the past. She was willing to never answered her phone when I called back to tell her to get on the train meet me at Silver Spring Station.

She called me 5 or 6 times, the last time I got a call from her. I figured that she needed some money and was willing to come and help me this time, but. I did not feel like getting up and doing some work. I was enjoying my sleep and did not feel like being bothered. I wish I had answered her call, because I don't know if things would have turned different if I had let her come and stay with me for a couple of days and help me with my book orders. She ended up going somewhere. Nobody knew where she was.

I got a call from her sister who was worried because no one had heard from her in a couple weeks by that time. I myself had called her few times after she last called me, but the calls went straight to her answering service. She also had called her sister for the last time the same day, or a day before, or after she tried to reach me. Her case manager had not heard from her as well, in the same time period. The police were informed. They issued a missing person alert.

I decided to, with her sister's permission, to make missing person flyers for my friend Rhonda.

I designed a flyer on my laptop and went to FedEx Office in downtown Silver Spring to print at least a hundred copies of the flyer. I spent more time posting the flyers on the street than selling my books on the street as I had planned to do at that time. Sometimes, I went out with her sister, from places to places, to post flyers and also asked around homeless camps and places if anybody had seen her. I spent a lot of nights riding my bike from one part of town to another, and posted flyers on every street I travelled on.. One night, I started around 11pm in Silver Spring, on Georgia Avenue near the border with Washington DC and rode my bike all the way down Georgia avenue to downtown Washington DC, posting flyers on Electric poles mostly, but also on surfaces where passers-by could see the posters. I flooded the entire Trinidad neighborhood and other neighborhoods of North West and North East Washington DC. The flyers had her family contact phone number, as well as the police detective's, in case someone saw her and wanted to call.

On October 27, 2020, at about 9:30pm. I received a text message and phone calls from her sister informing me that she has just talked to her. She told her that she went out of town with friends, because she was stressed and wanted to clear her mind. Somebody, as she alleges, saw the flyers and contacted her. Now, I am not going to get into her personal business. But I tried to understand why she would just leave her apartment for a month and not say anything to anybody, including relatives, and not call or provide a number or contact, where she could be reached in case of emergency.

She claimed that she was in North Carolina with friends and got a call from a friend of hers in Washington DC, who informed her that they were flyers everywhere about her missing. I know she is a grown-up woman, who was about 42 years old, and had the right to travel or do whatever she wanted. But I was a little bit perplexed that she did not inform anybody including family and her case worker. Such a behavior may not make any sense to many of you. But I have seen it countless times, with people who are homeless or have been homeless. In my book Homeless Lives Matter, I gave examples of homeless acquaintances who got into housing but were still spending more time outside and even sleeping outside for days, weeks and months without going to their apartment. So, it takes time for some former homeless to readjust to living indoors after being homeless for a long time. I knew and heard of homeless acquaintances who had got housed in an apartment with rent paid for and furnished but who still lived in a tent or slept outside.

My friend Rhonda had been homeless for years and had just got her apartment few months earlier.

On November 3, 2020, I was on my way to sell my books when Rhonda's younger sister called me while crying on the phone and told me, that her sister was just found dead in her apartment. I rode my bike to the building and met her sister crying hysterically outside. I could not stop crying myself. It was so sad to see my friend being carried of the building in a body bag, about half an hour after I joined her sister and her sister's boyfriend, outside, in front of the building. The body was found by the maintenance guy according to her sister. It was decomposed beyond recognition. That meant that she died few days earlier, after she had talked to her sister. This was a very sad story to me. But this is a recurring reality that I have witnessed or known about, of people who have dealt with homelessness for so long. Even when they get housed, they are still not free from the reality of the streets.

I could not attend Rhonda funeral service because I had an eye doctor's appointment the same day, Tuesday 30th at same time. But I made a little contribution from my book sales. I was so proud of her younger sister, with whom I spent hours and days on the street looking for Rhonda. She was at the forefront of organizing this great tribute to her sister. The only problem I had was the Eulogy. A Eulogy to my understanding is to praise the deceased and show sympathy for the family. But, from what I heard in the video, I felt that my friend and anybody in her situation, was being convicted, judged and condemned by the Pastor of the church where the service was held. I thought the words of the Reverend were totally inappropriate for such an occasion. I know Rhonda. I knew that she was a victim of sex abuse from age 6 to age 8 by her mother's husband, who she called daddy although not a biological father. I know what she shared with me about her struggle as a result of being sexually victimized as a child.

I really am not here to write about other people's personal lives. But I refuse the stigmas that are attached to people who go through a hard life, and the blame on them living the way they do, as the result of the wrong that was done to them, when they were innocent children. It is easy to send everybody to hell for what we see wrong in their life, but you need to know what caused anybody to become homeless, or seek refuge in addiction, or depression.

I was really disturbed by those words. Maybe it was meant for me not to attend because I would have exteriorized my frustrations at those unkind words, by interrupting the Pastor and ask him if he was aware about the trauma that Rhonda has been suffering from and never healed from since childhood. Contrary to that reverend, I am convinced that no God will condemn my friend Rhonda for having gone through such a traumatic life since childhood. The person who deserves eternal punishment for their action is the so-called Reverend who stand on top of a dead woman in her casket and calls her a whore in front of her teenage kids and tell the audience that she is going to hell. This was the sickest thing I ever heard coming from the mouth of a so-called man of God. All I know about my good buddy Rhonda is that she was just a wonderful human being who never healed from being victimized. That is all I can say about her. May her soul continue to rest in peace.

When you see a person experiencing homelessness, addiction, mental illness or depression, have some compassion and empathy for them. and if you are your relatives, check on them regularly. Make sure that they have access to the help they need, instead of rejecting, judging, condemning of giving up on them. As in the case of my friend Rhonda, I have known and befriended many other female homeless whose life has been messed up because they have never been able to heal mentally from the sexual abuse from older relatives and parents that they suffer when they were children. They live with that trauma for the rest of their life.

I know another homeless lady who is my friend. She is 34 years old. I have known her since she was 21. She has been living in tents, abandominiums - as abandoned houses are called in the homeless vernacular- since I have known her. Her story is extremely sad. She has been sexually molested by her biological father since she was a child. Her father who is also homeless but in jail now, was still having sex with her until recently before he was jailed for assaulting some other homeless female. She told me that, when sometimes she falls asleep after getting high, her father would have sex with her while she was asleep. She told me that, one day, before her father was arrested for something else, he and her had an argument and he sets her tent on fire while she was in there. Luckily, she got out of there unharmed. Now, when people see a young female like that homeless, on drugs, caught up with the street life, their first reaction is that they like that kind of lifestyle and chose to be homeless. But people making this kind of judgement have no clue what kind of trauma these women have been through and have not healed from.

It is easy to blame others for their misery and suffering and believe that they made a conscious choice to be homeless and therefore deserve what they are going through, when you may not have any idea how much suffering and pain they are going through out there, never experienced what they go through and may not grasp the complexity and intricacies of their situation.

Fact of the matter is that every human being deserves a roof over his or her head and a place to call home, whether they have issues with addiction, unemployment, mental illness, or any other stereotypical issues that is noticeable among the homeless. No matter what issue we face in life, every human being deserves a roof over their head and a place to call home.

My Female Homeless Friend stabbed on the street corner

I was removing the missing person flyers for Rhonda, that I had posted on around North Capitol Street and Florida Avenue. Renee wobbled towards me with her lanky frame and stood in front of me. They found her, she said with a smile on her face. She was happy that her missing friend was finally found. Unfortunately, she did not know that I had just come from the building where Rhonda lived, and that her dead body was carried away in front of me and her sister, half an hour earlier. "Yes, they found her dead in her apartment a few hours ago" I told her. "No!", she yelled while tears gushed down her cheeks. "That was my friend", she uttered while crying. "They told me that they found her, and she was ok, and she came home" she said. I explained to her that, she did retuned home five days ago, but her dead decomposed body had just been found on the floor, next to his bed, by the maintenance guy, when he entered her apartment and smelled a strong and foul odor. I looked her in the eyes. She gazed at me as if she guessed that I was about to say something very serious to her. "You gonna be the next if you keep hanging around here" I said to her." She seemed chocked and disturbed to hear what I said. "I don't hang around here like that no more. I just got off the bus. I'm getting my place; I already got my voucher. I am moving to my own apartment two blocks from here. I already seen the place. They won't see me around here no more." She said defensively. Then she wrapped her hands around me and held me very tight for 30 seconds and gave me a kiss on the cheek." I found it very strange, although she held me a lot before. But I felt the intensity of her grip around my torso, this time. That was the last time I saw her before she got stabbed on the same spot a week later and died in the hospital, shortly after the ambulance took her to the emergency room. I didn't know that she was telling me goodbye, the way she held me and gave me that kiss on the cheek. She died the same day she had got her keys to her new apartment and a week after my other homeless friend died in the apartment, she was housed a couple of months earlier. I was very saddened that these two beautiful and wonderful friends of mine who have endured a hard life into homelessness died tragically, when they just got housed. Both of them had children. One had two teenage kids in the custody of her mother, and the other one had three, one teenager and two little kids in the custody of their father. I found out about her death three days later, after she got stabbed. But the same day that she got killed, I went to the camp where she had her tent. It was the park on New Jersey Avenue, near a fire station and across Dunbar High school, a reputed high school in Washington DC. I rode my bike there to check on her. Her other friend, the one I wrote about earlier whose tent got set on fire by her father, told me that Renee had just left on the way to the spot where I last talked to her. Her friend was concerned about Renee hanging around that spot. She thought it was too much going on around there with the folks hanging around there. She told me that Renee had just got her keys and handed her, her tent and all her belongings, because she was moving in her new apartment the same day. I was very happy for her. I left. Three days later, I was told by another homeless female that Renee got stabbed by a guy known as Gorilla T. I later was told by other homeless buddies that she was fighting another female and had got on top of her while beating her. The guy Gorilla T pulled a knife and stabbed Renee more than ten times in her pelvic and vagina area.

What happened to her did not make any sense to me. I really loved her as a person. I heard so many bad things about her being a violent person, but in my presence, she was an angel and sweet person. I used to stop and talk to her all the time when I rode my bike from my tent to SOME to take a shower. She was hanging around with other homeless folks on the corner of Florida Avenue and North Capitol street. She was drinking a lot and fussing a lot as well when she was drunk. But anytime she saw me, she just got up or moved away from her friends and walked up to me. Me and her will walk away most of the time, toward the liquor store. She always asked me to buy her a drink. I never refused. I talked to her while we walked slowly. We stopped a lot of time on the way so that she could talk to me. I listened to her talking about her life and her plan to get out of her situation and do better. Many times, I admonished her when she told me that she had got into a fight with someone. She was 32 years old. I used to tell her she was beautiful and intelligent and had a lot of potential and should get herself out of the street. She wanted to come and help me with processing and packing my books, but I never showed up anytime I was supposed to come and get her. She always begged me to let her read my books, but I never brought her a copy.

I don't know how she ended up into homelessness, but I thought she deserved better. Her tragic end on the same day she got her keys to her own place is beyond me. What really got me to address her case in this book is that no serious efforts were made by the police to arrest the person who killed her. Her name is still listed in the Washington Metropolitan Police Department 2021 unsolved homicides. The homeless who frequented the area at the time, knew who killed her. The guy was a homeless man himself who was sleeping in a tent few blocks from the area. He himself got stabbed a two months later a block away and died on the scene if I am not mistaken.

I can write an entire book with more examples of homeless female friends of mine who ended tragically, while they were homeless or few months after they got out of homelessness.

Although, I cannot claim to understand the circumstances of each and all homeless individuals that I have met and known through my own decades-long journey through homelessness, I can say that people are homeless for reasons deeper than a simple desire and choice to be homeless. I understand homelessness from personal experience and familiarity with the reality of other homeless who I have met, known, or befriended.

This is why I want you to be less judgmental and instead have more compassion and empathy for the homeless that you see out there.

If you have a relative experiencing homelessness, addiction, mental illness or depression, check on them regularly and make sure they have access to the help they need instead of rejecting, judging and condemning of giving up on them.

HOMELESSNESS NOT A CHOICE

CHAPTER 8

GETTING PUT OUT, DON'T KNOW WHAT TO DO

Landlord asked me to leave:

As a homeless activist, or anti homelessness activist to be correct, since I am no longer homeless and hopefully will never be again, I am constantly asked what the solution to homelessness is. The solution to homelessness is housing, period. To me housing is a human right. No human being deserves to be homeless. Every human being is entitled to a place to call home. Housing is a human right as far as I am concerned. One of the issues that I want to address in this last chapter is how landlord and tenant issues can contribute to homelessness. I know there are great landlords out there like my current landlord, who are doing right by their tenants, as long as the tenants are paying their rent, keeping everything peaceful and taking care of the place that they are renting. But there are also landlords who are only interested in rent money but do not take care of the property. They also do take advantage of their tenants and make things difficult for them. Those landlords, or slumlords, as they are called in Washington DC street vernacular, are not helping to solve homelessness. If anything, they are contributing to homelessness by putting tenants in a terrible predicament.

"Leo, I need to come upstairs and talk to you" My landlord said on the phone, when she called me the afternoon of October 25th, 2022. I knew it was not good news, that I was about to hear. "I am sorry I'm putting everybody out" she said, as soon as I opened the door and let her in.

I was asked by landlord to leave within 30 days. I could not believe this. I tried so hard to keep a roof over my head, after getting myself out of homelessness and paying my rent faithfully for nearly two years. And now, I was confronted with homelessness again, unless I could find a place as soon as possible to move in urgently, two days before my birthday.

I had no idea what I was going to do. I loved the place. I lived there for nearly 2 years. I moved there on February 1st, 2021. She sat down at my table, put a handwritten piece of paper on it and asked me to sign it. I read it.

It said:

"Notice to vacate, 10/25/2022.

30 Day notice to vacate your unit at XXXXX Wildwood Drive Silver Spring, MD 20905. I will use half of your deposit to pay for November rent. The remainder half will be mailed to your forwarding address within 30 days of your departure. Thank you. Pamela Cooper (I am not using her real name)."

I was dumbfounded and couldn't think of what to tell her right away because I was not in the mood to sign this.

"I am sorry, but I have to sell the house. And the folks who are buying it are waiting for this notice right now. I need you to sign it so I can call them now. They are waiting." She said with tears in her eyes. "I didn't want to sell the house, but I had to. I don't have 40 thousand dollars to do the repairs for the violations that the housing code inspector cited me for. So, I had to sell. I didn't make any money of it. I sold it for $200,000 less than it is worth I took a loss". She said.

"I need some time before signing this. You are asking me to move within a month by November 25, which is two days before my birthday." I responded.

"Look I am so sorry about that. I will give you good recommendations. You got to sign it, the folks are waiting", she said again.

"Sorry, I can't sign it right now. I need to have somebody look at it and let me know if this is correct" was my response.

"I'm supposed to give you guys 30 days", she interjected.

I knew that was some bull crap. From what I knew, it was supposed to be a 60 day instead of a 30-day notice to vacate. I told her. "I got to have somebody look at it" She got infuriated and told me "You make me regret to have rented you this place. "You were homeless, and nobody wanted to rent to you, but I did and now you are doing this to me?" she said. I didn't like her saying this to me. I thought that was not nice. I thought about all the rent money she made and the extra money she was getting off me, by making me pay too much for the utilities. I knew she was cheating me, but I just paid her whatever she was telling the utility bills were and never complained. But I kept my composure although I was getting upset as well. And I kind of felt that this notice was not proper and would not hold in the court of law. I told her, "Ok, I'm gonna sign it, but you got add on it the reason why you are giving me this notice". She said ok. She grabbed it and added" The reason for everyone moving out is because the house has been sold. ". I grabbed it back, read and signed it.

A week earlier, on October 18, 2022, a team of housing code enforcement of the Montgomery County Department of Housing and Community Affairs (DHCA), came and did a full inspection of the property. They cited the landlord for 12 violations of the Montgomery County Code concerning smoke alarm installation, a condemned structure, electrical wiring for entire facility and the exterior, permit for an attached dwelling, maintenance of the yard, interior walls constructed without permit, presence of several vehicles and trailers without tags on the property and presence of solid waste (tarps, branches, appliances, plastic, broken furniture, lawn mowers in disrepair, scattered outside on the property. A reinspection was supposed to be conducted a month later on November 22, 2022. The citation also said "Failure to properly correct these violations may result in the issuance of a civil citation for each offense. The offense(s) will be prosecuted in the District Court of Maryland for Montgomery county. The penalty provisions may include the imposition of a civil fine of up to $1000 for each violation. 3 days later, on October 21, she sent me this message at 9;59am: "We have a contractor coming Monday at noon to look at the work required by the county." And on October 24, 6 days after the inspection, she sent me a message at 8;36 Am, to remind me that the contractor will be there at noon and that I should leave my door unlocked if I was not going to be home. I was suspicious about what you were telling me because I suspected that she was going to sell the house instead of doing the repairs.

The unit underneath me was condemned by the lead inspector a month, prior to the full inspection that she conducted on the 18 of October. She came unannounced early that morning and went into that unit. The occupant of the unit was a 62- or 63-year-old lady with serious health issues and was walking with a cane. He was living in a unit in the basement. The basement was divided into two units with separate entrances and separated by a wall that the landlord build. That was the main reason why the unit was condemned because it was a violation of the housing code. The house was a single-family home that the owner turned into a multi dwelling housing, without the county permission and in violation of the county housing code. My unit was a two-bedroom apartment. The two units in the basement had a bedroom, a kitchen area and a bathroom in each of them. The owner also built another three-bedroom apartment on top of the garage. She turned the garage into a one-bedroom apartment. She and her husband stayed in there half of the year in the spring and summer before going back to their main residence in Florida, in the Winter each year. The older gentlemen, 72 years old who rented the unit above the garage, lived there for 11 years. He was living there alone with his two cats.

The lady below me was obese, about 400 to 450 pounds. She was having a hard time bringing her groceries in from her car. She had to take a bag or two at a time. One day, I heard her moaning and crying while in the door way at the entrance of the house, below the steps to my door and above the steps to hers below me. I opened my door and helped her by going to her car and taking the rest of her groceries back to her basement unit. I told her that from then on, all she had to do is let me know when she had to go to the grocery store, and I would come out and take her groceries to her apartment for her if I was home. I did that all the time she texted or knocked on my door to let me know that she was driving to the store and would text me or blow her horn when she was back. She did not carry her phone with her most of the time.

One evening, I heard her screamed outside repeatedly "Leo, I need help". I was in my living room which is at the back side of the house. I walked to my bedroom which was on the front ride side of the house, on the same side as the walkway. I looked through my window and saw her on the ground unable to get up. I walked outside and tried to lift her up, but I was not able to. She was way too heavy for me. She asked me to help her crawl to her car and then try to get her to get in her car seat. I grabbed the metal chair that was in the yard and put it in front of her and helped her crawled by moving the chair few steps at a time. It took us about 10 minutes to get her to her car, but I could not help her get in her car seat after several trials. I told her that I had to call emergency because there was no other option. Three firemen showed up within minutes. They tried and could not lift her up. They called for backup. Four or five more showed up. They were 7 or 8 of them. They tried several times and got up the ground to a chair that they had behind her. They got her up and had her hold her cane while they helped her walk to her unit in the basement. Things got worse since then. She was constantly crying and screaming late in the night because she was in pain. I don't know exactly what ailment she was suffering from but, I was very concerned. One day, she screamed and cried all night. Early in the morning, I called the landlord to tell her to go check on her. The landlord was in town and staying in her garage turned into an apartment. It was about 7 am. She went down there and ended up calling for an ambulance. But the lady downstairs refused to go the hospital.

A few days later, she started screaming my name for help again. I went downstairs to her bedroom window. She was on the floor. She said she felt and wanted me to come in to help her get up. I knew I couldn't, but I went to her door, but it was locked. I told her that I could not get inside because the door was locked. She asked me to get through the window. I told her, no, I could not do that, but I would call 911 instead. I called the emergency number and firemen and an ambulance showed up immediately. They went downstairs and got her and wanted to take her to the hospital, but she refused. Hours later in the evening, she started screaming for help again because she fell one more time. I went downstairs and convinced her to go to the hospital because her condition was worsening. She needed to be under constant medical care. I asked for her sister's number and called her sister so we can talk to her. I put my phone on the speaker and stood by her door so she could hear her sister talk to her. She agreed to go to the hospital. I called emergency and they sent an ambulance and an army of firemen. They picked her up and carried her on a stretcher to the ambulance. She was back in her apartment a week later. I called her sister and told her that she needed to go to a assisted living facility where she would get the care she needs because staying in the basement was no longer safe for her. I even said something to the landlord to that effect. It was clear that the lady should no longer stay in that basement by herself after falling on the floor repeatedly and having the ambulance come several times back-to-back. But nobody took me seriously. She started screaming again early in the morning around 6 am a couple of days after she returned to her basement unit. She kept hollering "I wanna to go home, I am cold, I don't have any blanket, I am hungry, I wanna go home, help, help!" I ignored her for a while because I was sleeping and was kind of used to her screaming all night but refuse to go to the hospital when we call emergency and an ambulance show up." But I started being concerned and went downstairs. She asked me for a blanket. I went upstairs and got one but when I came back downstairs, she was not able to open the door. She said she was on the floor and had no clothes on and kept saying she wanted to go home. It was obvious to me that she was a state of delirium. Also, she said that she had no clothes on, she was cold, she was on the floor, and she wanted to go home. So, I called emergency. They came and had a hard time getting in. They took her to the hospital. She stayed there for 3 or 4 days and came back to her apartment in the basement, one night with her sister. I left in the morning to go sell my books on the streets in downtown Washington DC. I got home late at night. I opened the front door and entered the house. But I saw a notice posted on her door. The posted notice said "These Premises Are Condemned As Unfit For Human Habitation In Accordance With Section 13 of Montgomery County Housing And Building Maintenance Standards, Chapter 26, Montgomery County Code 2002. It is Illegal To Occupy tr To Permit a Person to Occupy These Premises Until the Department of Housing and Community Affairs Releases the Condemnation. DO NOT REMOVE THIS PLACARD! There was another form taped to the door as well. It says Emergency Field Notice. It listed the reason why the unit was condemned. I think the firemen reported to county code enforcement that they were no emergency entrance to the unit and that the windows were too tight for them to get in with their equipment. That led to the Housing Code inspector coming in and condemn the unit below me. She came later to conduct a full inspection of the entire property and cited the owner for 10 code violations.

Getting Put Out And About To Be Homeless Again

Two cars and a van pulled up and parked off the road by the entrance of the property near the mailbox. It was obvious to me that these folks were not contractors as the landlord told me. My guess was that they were there to purchase the property. I called the other tenant in the unit in the back side of the basement to let her know that the contractors had arrived. The landlord met them outside and showed them the property starting on the yard front and back. The other tenant in the basement that I had called came outside and went to the street to look at the name of the company on the van. I was watching her through my window while talking to her on the phone and she read the name of the company to me on the phone. I checked them out online. It was a construction company that built houses. That confirmed my suspicions. That was on October 24th. 6 days after the inspection. It was the next day, on October 25th, that she came to tell me that she was putting all of us out. That meant that the so-called contractors decided to buy the house right after they did a walk through a day earlier. Now she wanted us to leave within a month when the cold weather and winter was about to start and also a day after thanksgiving, which was on Thursday November 24th. It is by no means my intention to judge the landlord. But she herself wanted me to sign a 15 month lease, from February 2021 to April 2022 instead of a 12 month lease from February 2021 to January 2022, because she didn't want to worry about trying to rent the place in the winter in case I decided to move out after my lease time was completed. She said she'd rather do that in the Spring. But now, she wanted us to move out in the winter in the holiday season. She sold the house and made her money and did not have to worry about the inspections.

I personally did not think that I would leave on November 25th, which was two days before my birthday. I got online and spent days and nights searching for a place. She closed on the house sale on Monday November 22, 2022, and left town. But earlier that day, the new owners who own a construction company located in Bethesda, Maryland, came to do a last walk through. I was expecting them to come and knock on my door because the landlord had informed me of that last walk through by the buyers. I left my door unlocked while waiting in the bedroom. But I heard the door being opened without a knock. I rushed outside the bedroom and saw a man standing inside. "Who are you?" I asked him. "I am the new owner" he said and added" You supposed to leave by the end of this month. When are you leaving? "You have to come and talk to us" I said to him while the landlord and two of the owner's partners were coming up the stairs. He totally ignored me and said with arrogance "I am demolishing this place on December 1st". "Do what you got to do!" I quipped. I knew he was not going to be able to do any demolition on the property without a permit and I did not think he could get a permit to demolish it that soon. The landlord had also texted me, few days ago to tell me that she wanted to collect the cable TV box and the internet modem and also that she will cut the utilities (water, electricity, and gas) on November 27. I told her that my birthday was on November 27. She told me that she will wait till the 28th to cut electricity, Gas and Water. I really couldn't believe that the landlord and the new owner were trying to use fear tactics to get us out there.

She left town in the evening of November 21, after she closed the deal on the house. The other tenants and I were not concerned by the imminent expiration on November 25th of the handwritten notice to vacate she gave us. We kept in contact with the Housing code enforcement officer and kept her informed about the transaction. She was supposed to come back on November 22 to follow up with the inspection. She contacted the landlord and asked him to give us a proper notice to vacate conformed to the Montgomery county landlord tenant laws. What the previous landlord gave us was a piece of trash. She should have given us a 60-day notice to vacate, and the notice should start on the first of the month. Her was a 30-day notice starting on the 25th of October. Also, she put on the notice that she was going to use half of the security deposit to apply it towards November rent. Security deposits are not to be used for rent by landlords.

On November 23, a day before thanksgiving day, I received the following text message from landlord after she sold the house and left town, "I just forwarded you each an email from the new owners." I was confused because the new owners were now our landlord and should contact us themselves. I was even more shocked when I read the following email sent on Wednesday November 23, 2022.

"Hi XXXXXXXXX

Could you please deliver this notice to the Tenants

This is to notify you that as of today November 21, 2022, XXXXXX LLC

Has become the new owner of

XXXXXXX, Silver Spring MD. 20905.

Please vacate the property no later than November 25, 2022, as previously notified. Our company will begin clearing the home by November 26, 2022, anything left on the premises will be removed by our crew in order to begin demolition."

I called the new owner on the phone number of his company. He responded by reiterating the threats in the email. I told him that we needed more time to move out. He asked me how much time we needed. I told him that we needed till after the holiday season. That meant after Thanksgiving, Christmas, and the 1st of January of the new year, 2023. He got irritated and told me that if we don't leave by the end of the month, our property will be thrown out and the place bulldozed on December 1, 2022. He also mentioned that the previous landlord was going to cut off utilities. I asked him if he was going to restore it, his answer was negative. He said that he did not rent to us, and he has nothing to do with us and that he purchased the property, and we should just leave. I decided to end the conversation. I was sincerely worried that he and the former owners were going to cut off utilities to bully us out of there. We contacted the housing inspector. She wrote to the new owners and told him that it would be a violation to cut utilities while the tenants are still living there and that he would be fined if that happens. And also, she will get utilities restored within 48 hours.

I decided as an activist to share the issue on my social media platform to get some support and to get some pressure on the new owners so that they won't get us out of there by force. Many of my followers made phone calls to the Construction company number and reached out to elected officials in the county.

Some young activists showed at the house on the day that the construction company said that they were coming to start demolition preparation on the property. The elected county council member for the area contacted me after someone shared my post on Instagram with her. She reached out to the new owner as well and told him to issue us a new notice to vacate. The new owners ignored everybody asking them to issue us a notice to vacate. But they left us alone because obviously they faced too much pressure from all sides. Some of the tenant rights advocacy activists who came to support us, helped us get a lawyer from a local organization supporting tenants' rights.

The lawyer called us and informed us that the new owner filed a complaint to court on November 28, 2022, for holding over. The lawyer told us that he was confident that we would win the case because we were never issued a proper notice to vacate. He also told us that we should not pay any rent to new owners unless they show us a Montgomery county license to lease. We knew that the property would not pass inspection that would be required before a license to rent is issued to new owners. We also were told by lawyer that previous landlord did not have license to rent. One of the tenants lived there for 11 years, I was there for 2 years, and the other tenant rented there for 3 years.

According to the Maryland Court of Appeal, "If an unlicensed rental property was in good condition and the tenant voluntarily paid rent to an unlicensed landlord without any collection efforts by the landlord, the tenant cannot sue to get those rent payments back. However, if the unlicensed property was in disrepair, the tenant may have a cause of action for damages, including potentially partial or full repayment of rental payments.

Regardless of the condition of the unlicensed rental property, if the tenant does not pay rent for any unlicensed period, any efforts to collect such rent, regardless of whether the landlord has subsequently obtained a license, is prohibited under the Maryland Consumer Debt Collection Act."

The new owner had to wait until May 8 for the court to try the case they filed against me and another tenant. The third tenant case has not been scheduled yet. I was lucky enough to find a place in later November, but I kept some of my belongings to the old apartment in solidarity with the other two tenants. My unit is the main dwelling of the house. One tenant is in the basement and the other one in a unit built on top of the garage. I felt like if I moved out before the other two get a place, the new owners would access the main part of the house and make it hell for the other two. The issue is being resolved with our lawyer negotiating with the new owners' lawyers so that we can get our deposit back if we agree to move out by a date agreed on by both parties.

I used to ride through this neighborhood from my tent every morning, whenever I had to go take a shower to places providing services to the homeless, or when I had to go downtown to sell my books or go to grocery stores. I always fantasized about living one day in this neighborhood. I miraculously got a place to rent in the ideal place that I used to dream about in my dreams. The place cost me about twice what I used to pay for in my old apartment. That means that I have to sell twice as many books as I needed to sell monthly to make rent money. But, at least, I do not have to catch the train and bus before getting home an hour later. Now, I can catch 3 different buses from the place where I sell my books to my new place after a 10-minute ride. There is a metro station 10 minutes' walk away, and I can ride my bike to several grocery stores in 5 minutes. I try to be a good person and it feels like things always work for the better no matter what I go through. I am not complaining, I am grateful. Leo